ORAL TRADITION

ORAL
TRADITION

*A Modern Problem in Old Testament
Introduction*

EDUARD NIELSEN

With a Foreword by
H. H. ROWLEY

SCM PRESS LTD
56 BLOOMSBURY STREET
LONDON

First published 1954
Second impression 1955
Third impression 1958
Fourth impression 1961

Printed in Great Britain by
Robert Cunningham and Sons Ltd
Longbank Works, Alva

CONTENTS

FOREWORD

MUCH has been written in recent years about the Scandinavian traditio-historical school which has its headquarters in Uppsala, and whose most forceful leader is Professor Engnell. Unfortunately the work in which Professor Engnell has given the fullest account of its methods and results, his *Gamla Testamentet: en traditionshistorisk inledning*, is but half published in Swedish. The unpublished second volume appears to have been seen by a number of other Scandinavian scholars, and is frequently referred to, but the promised English translation of the already published volume is not yet within sight of publication. The articles by Engnell and others in the *Svenskt Bibliskt Uppslagsverk* indicate the positions of the school on most questions, but are again available only in Swedish. When, therefore, I learned that Mr. E. Nielsen, who had published three articles on Oral Tradition in the *Dansk Teologisk Tidsskrift* in 1952, was ready to translate them into English, it seemed to me desirable that this should be done, so that readers who had no access to the Scandinavian tongues should be able to understand more clearly the aim and method of the school. So far as I know these articles, which are now gathered together here with some additional material, offer a better introduction to traditio-historical criticism than can be found elsewhere in any of the international languages of scholarship.

That I am not myself an adherent of the new school does not affect my readiness to welcome its presentation to English readers. New points of view should be given an opportunity of expression, and students should be given the opportunity to form their own judgement on them. While, therefore, I am still a literary critic—though not, I hope, with a closed mind against new solutions of our problems, and ready to modify the older solutions at a number of points without repudiating the older method in the same thoroughgoing, and almost scornful, manner that is characteristic of the new school—I have gladly given much time and trouble to further this presentation in an English dress of the views of the Scandinavian scholars.

For the content of the translation I have no responsibility. That was prepared in Denmark—partly by Mr. Nielsen himself and partly under his supervision. The translation was in general good and readable, but I made a large number of minor changes to make the English read more smoothly, and made many small changes in the form of the work. That the translation has a slightly foreign flavour is inevitable and is no disadvantage to the reader. So long as the meaning is clear—and I have endeavoured to see that that is so—he will have little cause for complaint; if he wishes to be difficult, he may prefer to learn Danish and read it in the original. My own access to Danish is not free, and I have confined myself to recourse to the original for any changes that I have made, where I have been in any doubt. These changes have been submitted to Mr. Nielsen, and the whole has also been read through by Professor G. W. Anderson, who has a thorough knowledge of the Scandinavian languages. It is my hope, therefore, that the final result is an accurate rendering, which will not be displeasing, and which will enable students to judge for themselves how far the new methods can supplement the old and how far they can successfully replace them.

H. H. ROWLEY

Manchester University

AUTHOR'S PREFACE

THE present work is a collection of articles, published in *Dansk Teologisk Tidsskrift*, xiii (1950) and xv (1952). In these articles I have tried to present to the readers of this periodical an introduction to the modern problem of oral tradition together with some analyses of Old Testament traditions, illustrating, I hope, that literary criticism is not the only legitimate scientific approach to the texts of the Old Testament.

These articles are now introduced to a larger public. That this has been possible is wholly due to the kind efforts of Professor H. H. Rowley, who has spent much time and labour on my MS. I wish to express my deepest gratitude towards a scholar, who belongs to the circles of literary criticism and nevertheless is endowed with an almost patriarchal magnanimity, in that he has given time and trouble to further a work which tries to combat literary criticism.

The fundamental views of these articles are characteristic of the traditio-historical 'school', I think. They are at any rate greatly inspired by the views of Pedersen, Nyberg and Engnell. My detailed exegesis of, e.g., Gen. 6-9 or Mic. 4-5 is of course entirely my own.

Finally I express my gratitude to my translator, Miss Asta Lange, M.A., for the skill with which she has carried out her difficult task, and to the Rask-Ørsted Foundation for its support of the translation.

EDUARD NIELSEN
*Universitetsadjunkt at the University
of Aarhus*

*Aarhus,
March 30th 1953*

ABBREVIATIONS

A. f.O.	*Archiv für Orientforschung.*
A.N.E.T.	*Ancient Near Eastern Texts.*
A.O.T.	*Altorientalische Texte zum Alten Testament.*
G.-B.	Gesenius-Buhl, *Hebräisches und aramäisches Handwörterbuch über das Alte Testament.*
J.A.O.S.	*Journal of the American Oriental Society.*
K.A.R.	*Keilschrifttexte aus Assur religiösen Inhalts.*
K.B.	Keilinschriftliche Bibliothek.
M.V.A.G.	*Mitteilungen der vorderasiatischen Gesellschaft.*
N.T.T.	*Norsk Teologisk Tidsskrift.*
R.A.	*Revue d'Assyriologie et d'Archéologie orientale.*
R.B.	*Revue biblique.*
R.H.R.	*Revue de l'histoire des religions.*
S.A.T.	Die Schriften des Alten Testaments in Auswahl.
S.E.Å.	*Svensk Exegetisk Årsbok.*
T.C.L.	*Textes cunéformes du Louvre.*
U.U.Å.	Uppsala Universitets Årsskrift.
V.A.B.	Vorderasiatische Bibliothek.
V.A.S.	Vorderasiatische Schriftdenkmäler.
Z.A.W.	*Zeitschrift für die alttestamentliche Wissenschaft.*

I

INTRODUCTION

THE reader of the title of this book may possibly be astonished at the use of the word 'modern' in connection with 'oral tradition'. He knows very well that 'oral tradition' as a working hypothesis has played an important role in the history of Christian theology, and not only in Old Testament Introductions. The present generation of theologians will especially remember the rise of 'Form Criticism', primarily in Old Testament exegesis, and secondarily and later among New Testament scholars.

From the almost classic, but antiquated,[1] commentary on Genesis by Hermann Gunkel the reader will perhaps take the following example: 'On leisurely winter evenings the family sits by the fireside. The grown-ups and especially the children listen intently to the old and beautiful stories of the far past, which though heard so often are in unfailing demand. We enter and listen with them . . . '[2]

Furthermore the reader will possibly emphasize the fact that a scholar like Gunkel is particularly well able to reduce the oral tradition to its legitimate position. He does not abandon the literary-critical tradition of his Fatherland. On the contrary, in his commentary even the great emphasis he places on oral tradition has been combined with a minute dissection of the whole Pentateuch into four or more principal strands. These strands are thought to have come into existence as written sources at different epochs in the history of the development of Israelite culture. They are supposed to be distinct enough to be reconstructed—not always without some

---

[1] Antiquated, not only because of literary criticism and source-analysis with the consequent rearrangement of the material, but especially because the reader is constantly aware of the way in which the 'mature Western European' presents the naïve attitude of the 'childish Oriental' towards nature, his naïve moral code, his naïve conception of God, etc. It is the 'mature' Western European who is naïve in his feeling of cultural superiority.

[2] *Genesis*, 5th ed., 1922, p. xxxi.

difficulty—by the analytical work of the initiated investigator.[1]

To begin with we may emphasize the fact that when we speak of oral tradition as a *modern* problem in Old Testament research we do not intend to reduce oral tradition to a 'pre-literary stage'. For in this connection, especially after Gunkel's contributions, it is hardly possible to call the question of the role of oral tradition a *problem*. Already Wellhausen[2] had gone so far as to recognize the existence of oral tradition behind the individual legends of 'JE'. Budde[3] went further by supposing oral *compositions* of single legends, especially for 2 Sam. 9 ff, and Gunkel continued this trend in Old Testament research through his traditio-historical work. Behind the Pentateuch he supposed the existence of oral *cycles* of legends, partly composed in guilds of narrators. This point of view has been accepted, e.g., by A. Lods in his essay 'Le rôle de la tradition orale dans la formation des récits de l'Ancien Testament'.[4] The readers of Gunkel and Lods will doubtless agree that these two scholars are right in this, that even the cycles of legends must originate in oral tradition. But the attentive reader cannot escape the impression that another problem arises, the problem of the legitimacy of that literary criticism for which both these scholars stand,[5] faithful as they are to the tradition of Old Testament research. In other words, we are faced with the question of drawing a well-defined line between a literary and a pre-literary stage, belonging to a literary and an oral culture respectively.

When we speak of oral tradition as a *modern problem* we direct attention primarily to a series of contributions, chiefly Scandinavian, from the last decades, contributions which try to get rid of the assumption which in our culture, with its enthusiasm for writing and defective memory, has too often

[1] A view which is maintained in principle by the German traditio-historian M. Noth. Cf. his *Überlieferungsgeschichte des Pentateuchs*, 1948, esp. pp. 1-44.

[2] *Die Composition des Hexateuchs*, 1889, p. 9

[3] *Geschichte der althebräischen Literatur*, 1906, pp. 35 ff

[4] In R.H.R., lxxxviii, 1923, pp. 51 ff

[5] In this connection it is interesting to note that the learned clerical critics and reviewers of Jean Astruc's *Conjectures . . .*, 1753, were among the first to deny the validity of his criteria by referring to the narrative technique of the Orientals; cf. A. Lods, *Jean Astruc et la critique biblique au XVIII⁰ siècle*, 1924, pp. 64, 66

formed the starting point for scientific analysis of the traditions of antiquity.

H. S. Nyberg is the first of those who call for mention. The main purpose of his pioneering and epoch-making work *Studien zum Hoseabuche*[1] is to warn against, and to combat, a prevailing tendency among Old Testament scholars to surmount the difficulties of the Massoretic text, either by means of more or less arbitrary textual emendations, or by using the old translations, especially the Septuagint, without any clear method. But in addition the author also touches upon the question of oral tradition, its extent, its significance, and its reliability. Later we shall return to this important study, but for the present we content ourselves with sketching the progress of research.

Partly inspired by Nyberg, H. Birkeland[2] discusses the 'oral tradition' behind the Old Testament prophetical books. Birkeland like Nyberg stresses that Old Testament literature is a product of ancient oriental culture. Here writing is always secondary, used for the one purpose of preserving the oral message from destruction, whereas oral tradition is primary, creative, sustaining and shaping, a fact well-known especially from Arabian and Persian culture. The Dutch scholar, van der Ploeg,[3] has with some reason characterized this booklet, which in less than 100 pages tries to offer a new solution of the literary problems that are connected with all the Old Testament prophetical books, and moreover only *one* solution,[4] as *peu approfondi*. But in reality it is very meritorious to try to see from a completely new point of view material that has been worked over again and again.

In 1943 Mowinckel published a study, 'Oppkomsten av Profetlitteraturen',[5] in which he strongly stresses the fact that the prophets were men of the spoken word and that their books were compositions based on oral tradition. We owe it to oral

---

[1] *U.U.Å.*, 1935, No. 6
[2] *Zum hebräischen Traditionswesen* (Avhandlinger utgitt av det norske videnskaps-akademi i Oslo), 1938
[3] In 'Le rôle de la tradition orale . . . ', *R.B.*, liv, 1947, pp. 5-41
[4] 'Alles das erklärt sich leicht, wenn man die mündliche Tradition als Träger der Überlieferung ansieht,' etc., p. 90; cf. pp. 54, 61, 67, 81, etc.
[5] In *N.T.T.*, xlii, pp. 65-111

tradition, for instance, that the prophecies of Amos and Hosea were preserved until the exilic age, which was also the age when the prophecies were committed to writing. As to Isaiah we are directly informed how a 'complex of tradition' (a collection of oracles, related by form or subject-matter) is preserved and 'sealed up among his disciples' (Isa. 8.16).[1] As to the reliability of oral tradition Mowinckel is a little sceptical. He emphasizes oral tradition as a living process in which, for instance, the material is often reshaped and adapted to new situations. In this manner Mowinckel finds room for his well-known thesis advanced in *Jesaja-disiplene* (1926) where he dealt with the transformation of the pre-exilic prophecy of judgement to a nationalistic prophecy of happiness. This thesis is Birkeland's second source of inspiration for his above-mentioned work.

In 1945 Ivan Engnell published the first part of his *Gamla Testamentet: en traditionshistorisk inledning*,[2] a work planned on a generous scale. He tries to open new paths for research in Old Testament introduction, and his book is remarkable for a religio-historical orientation which has nothing in common with the prevalent 'evolutionistic'[3] conception of the religion of Israel. A whole chapter in the book (pp. 109-167) is devoted to this subject. His general views are too well-known to need any outline here. The outstanding feature of his book, however, is its vigorous repudiation of the still current method of literary criticism. At the same time he emphasizes the role of oral tradition, and stresses the anachronistic way in which modern Western-European science applied to texts from antiquity points of view that belong to the sixteenth to twentieth centuries. Even though he advances his point of view very forcefully Engnell is far from a rabid or blind insistence on a favourite hypothesis. On the contrary, like Nyberg, he emphasizes several times that the question of the existence and

---

[1] Understood in this way already by Gandz in 1935 (*Jewish Studies in Memory of G. A. Kohut*, pp. 248 f); cf. Engnell, *Gamla Testamentet*, i, 1945, p. 41, and his *Call of Isaiah*, 1949, p. 59, but questioned by Widengren, *Literary and Psychological Aspects*, 1948, pp. 69 ff
[2] Part II has not yet been published
[3] In the sense of steadily evolving from lower to higher levels

significance of oral tradition demands different answers for different kinds of literature.[1] Engnell has given a more varied study of the prophetical literature in his 'Profetia och Tradition',[2] a work that may be regarded as an answer to Mowinckel's *Prophecy and Tradition*,[3] published the same year.

The last-mentioned work by Mowinckel is a presentation of his above-mentioned article from the *Norsk Teologisk Tidsskrift* to a wider circle of readers. Here he defends his principal thesis from *Jesaja-disiplene*,[4] and accordingly emphasizes the element 'history' in 'history of tradition'.[5] It is also in part a reply to Engnell's *Gamla Testamentet*. The issue between Mowinckel and Engnell is whether the so-called 'positive oracles in the pre-exilic prophetical books', Amos, Hosea, Isaiah, and Micah, are to be considered original or secondary. Everyone who is acquainted with recent Old Testament exegesis will realize that this question has less to do with the problem of oral or written tradition than with the question of the relation of the prophets to the cult.

Of greater interest for our problem is Mowinckel's hypothesis of the genesis of the book of Jeremiah, to which we shall revert later. We have already said that Engnell's 'Profetia och Tradition' represented a more varied study of the problem of oral tradition in relation to Old Testament prophecy. Engnell divides the prophetical books into two types: 1. the liturgy-type, and 2. the dîwân-type, and thus considerably restricts the role of oral tradition in the case of prophetic liturgies (e.g. Joel, Nahum, Habakkuk), while insisting on its significance for the prophetic dîwâns[6] (e.g. Amos, Hosea, Isaiah, Jeremiah). It is certain, indeed, that oral tradition has played a considerable part in the composition and transformation of the material. We must be careful, however, to avoid

---

[1] *Op. cit.*, pp. 41 f, 88, 104 f, etc.   [2] *S.E.Å.*, 1947, pp. 110-139
[3] Avhandlinger utgitt av det norske videnskaps-akademi i Oslo, 1947
[4] Cf. above
[5] Hence the book defends the positions of older Old Testament scholars. For instance, the significance of Gunkel's traditio-historical contribution is emphasized, while the decisive contribution of Nyberg's *Studien zum Hoseabuche* is not sufficiently appreciated.
[6] This expression was introduced into Old Testament study by H. S. Nyberg in his above-mentioned work

being misled into setting the circle of disciples up against the master. Together they form an indissoluble whole, and this is also true as to ideology.[1]

The next work to which we must draw attention is Geo Widengren's *Literary and Psychological Aspects of the Hebrew Prophets*.[2] This is characterized by a distinct reserve on the question of oral tradition, and is notable for an interesting and thorough examination of the pre-Islamic and early-Islamic material. The author tries to establish the probability that oral and written tradition have gone hand-in-hand with one another, and that the written tradition was the prevailing one in its special *milieu*, that is, in the cities. For instance, Birkeland refers to the history of the origin of the Qurân in support of his own views concerning the role oral tradition played for the Old Testament prophetical books. To this Widengren replies that in all probability Mohammed not only contributed, directly or indirectly, to putting the Qurân into writing, but even made some interpolations in the text on different occasions himself.[3] And in the case of Mohammed and the Qurân we may see the typical Semitic way of publishing a literary work. Here the poet himself takes the initiative in having his words written down, but without creating a definitively completed book to which nothing could be added later. From Arabic literature Widengren passes to the Old Testament, and Jeremiah is presented as an almost exact parallel to Mohammed, only with this important difference, that in Widengren's opinion Jeremiah had no circle of disciples to preserve his words in their memories.

In another respect, also, Widengren's work is a reaction against the stressing of the role of oral tradition. Van der Ploeg in his criticism of Nyberg and Birkeland had referred to the neighbouring cultures of Palestine, the Egyptian and the Mesopotamian, with their great enthusiasm for writing. Widengren adds to this the ancient Phoenician literature, as it is known from the inscriptions of Byblos and the mythological texts from Ras Shamra.

[1] *Op. cit.*, p. 130   [2] *U.U.Å.*, 1948, No. 10
[3] e.g. Sura lxxiv 31-34. Cf. Widengren, *op. cit.*, pp. 49 f.

Engnell has replied to this double challenge from his colleague in an 'Additional Note' in his book *The Call of Isaiah*.[1] He refutes Widengren's somewhat surprising misunderstanding of Engnell's position,[2] and disputes the right to apply analogies from Mohammed's Qurân to the Old Testament prophetical books. In the first place the great interval of time must not be overlooked. Next it is reasonable to suppose that the dictation of the Qurân was due to Mohammed's wish to create a holy book, to make his own Moslems an *ahl-el-kitāb*, like the Jews and the Christians. As to the Ras Shamra texts Engnell maintains that Ugarit seems to have held a special position in Phoenicia, and observes that 'One should therefore not jump to conclusions based on the Ras Shamra material concerning written transmission in Israel'. 'Is it by mere chance', Engnell demands, 'that no analogous written texts whatever have been found in the archaeologically so well explored Israelite Palestine?'[3]

We have tried to sketch the rough outline of this current debate among Old Testament scholars, especially the Scandinavians. However, to bring the reader into more intimate contact with the problem of oral tradition, we shall now try (1) to set forth some fundamental points of view concerning the problem, illustrating this by means of testimonies from the ancient world outside the Old Testament, (2) to examine the role of oral tradition in the different kinds of Old Testament literature, and (3) to give some examples of the way in which the traditio-historical school treats texts from the Old Testament.

[1] *U.U.Å.*, 1949, No. 4, pp. 54 f
[2] In view of the outline of Engnell's position given above, it is strange that Widengren should maintain that Engnell has pushed Nyberg's ideas to the extreme and thus laid bare the weakness of the position (p. 8), and should say that it does not seem possible to proceed further in that line than Engnell has gone (p. 9)
[3] *Op. cit.*, p. 58

II

ORAL TRADITION IN
THE NEAR EAST

THE following chapter may be divided into four parts, dealing with (*a*) the value attributed to oral tradition in antiquity, contrasted with the 'normal' value which we with our present culture attribute to it; (*b*) the use made of oral tradition in antiquity, contrasted with the 'normal' use of it in our present culture; (*c*) the interplay between oral and written tradition; and (*d*) the difference between oral and written tradition illustrated by the variations that are characteristic of oral and written tradition respectively.

(*a*) As to the value of oral tradition we are in a favoured position in that texts have been preserved from antiquity, both from the Semitic and the non-Semitic worlds, which, directly or indirectly, bear witness to the importance attributed to oral tradition. These testimonies are in marked contrast to modern, rather sceptical, conceptions of oral tradition, especially with regard to its reliability. This naturally depends on the small use now made of oral tradition. Nowadays oral tradition is normally a living force only in degenerate forms, as for instance in slander. Hans Christian Andersen's fairy-tale of the hen who dropped a feather one evening when preening her feathers to please the cock, and then the next morning heard the scandal of the five hens who had plucked all their feathers off and so died of cold, takes off the current attitude to our problem. Bernhard Stade writes in his famous and still very instructive *Geschichte des Volkes Israels*:[1] '. . . it is a fact established by experience that information about ancestors based on oral tradition goes back at the most through three, usually only two generations.' Julius Wellhausen makes the following statement in his *Prolegomena*:[2] 'Only the separate stories are derived from popular tradition'—by this Wellhausen means

[1] Vol. i, 1887, p. 28   [2] Here quoted from 6th ed. p. 294

18

oral tradition—'and these stories are put into relation with
each other quite haphazardly; their combination into an inte-
grated unit is due to poetic or literary activity. The harmony
between the sources ... is only explained by literary dependence.' This statement refers to 'die Ursage der Genesis'.
Hugo Gressmann, who is well known for his contribution to
research dealing with Old Testament traditions, bears the
following testimony:[1] 'Only by written transmission is history
secured against complete disintegration into legends.' Nowadays we consult the documents, and the nearer a written
source is to its subject the more confident is its investigator.
In our present-day cultural circumstances this is the only possible attitude, when it is a matter of research concerning events
that lie within our own culture. Here it is legitimate to be on
one's guard against oral tradition. But this scepticism, legitimate *per se*, must not be applied as a matter of course to fields
with a *milieu* of genuine, living, oral tradition, whether these
fields are to be found in the ancient world or in our own time,
whether the culture is Semitic or Aryan.

The modern contempt for learning by heart—learning things
by heart is a necessary basis for oral tradition—is not exactly
characteristic of the ancient Semites. The ancient Mesopotamian culture seems to have been enthusiastic about writing;
but we have some texts that stress the importance attached to
learning by heart. From the often quoted conclusion of the
Irra-myth we cite:[2]

III,20	(amēl) ṭupšarru ša iḫ-ḫa-zu i-si-ti i-na nak-ri i-kab-bit ...	The scribe who learns this text by heart escapes the enemy, is honoured [in his own land]
21	ina a-šir-ti um-ma-ni a-šar ka-a-a-an šu-me i-zak-ka-ru	In the congregation of the learned where my name is constantly spoken
22	u-zu-un-šu a-pi-it-ti	I will open his ears.[3]

[1] *Die älteste Geschichtsschreibung in Israel*, 1921, p. 14
[2] The text is taken from Jensen, *K.B.* VI, i, p. 72
[3] Cf. the translations of Jensen (ibid., ina aširti ummāni = im Tempel des
Volk(heer)s), Ebeling (*A.O.T.*, 2nd ed., p. 230) and Oppenheim (*Orientalia*, xix,

In Ashurbanipal's prayer to Shamash, notable because it concludes with a curse and a benediction, somewhat similar to ancient oriental royal inscriptions, we read in the benediction:[1]

| rev. 8 | ša kam-mu an-na-a ih̬-h̬a-zu u-šar-ra-h̬u DI.KUD DINGIR. MEŠ.ᵈUTU | Whosoever shall learn this text [by heart] [and] glorify the judge of the Gods, Shamash |
| 9 | ... šu li-ša-qir-šu e-piš pi-i-šu MUH̬ UN.MEŠ li-ṭib | may he make his ... precarious, may the word of his mouth please the people.[2] |

To conclude we quote from tablet VII of Enuma Elish, which deals with the fifty names of Marduk:

146	en-qu mu-du-u mit-h̬a-riš lim-tal-ku	The sage and the learned shall together ponder [them],
147	li-ša-an-ni-ma a-bu ma-ri li-ša-h̬i-iz	father shall tell [of them] to son and teach [them to] him,
148	ša (amēl) re'i u na-qi-di li-pat-ta-a uz-na-šu-un	the ears of the shepherd and the herdsman shall be opened ...

The poem characteristically concludes with the following:

| 158 | tak-lim-ti mah̬-ru-u id-bu-bu pa-nu-uš-šu | ... this tradition that an old man had related in days long ago [he wrote down, |
| 159 | [iš-ṭur-ma iš-ta]-kan a-na te-re-ti ur-kiš | and] left it as an instruction to coming generations.[3] |

No. 2, p. 157, who translates: 'And the scholar who knows (it by heart, or who has learnt its interpretation), if also slighted in foreign countries, shall become important in his own—and I shall give him inspiration (lit. open his ears) in the assembly of the learned men where they assiduously mention my name.' And he interprets the words 'isiti ina nakri' (ibid., p. 158) as follows: 'One is inclined to think that the writer of our group of verses wished to express his thanks to the deity whose help and assistance has made him achieve importance in his native country after apparently experiencing failure abroad'). The verb 'ah̬āzu' is discussed by Widengren, *op. cit.*, p. 91, n. 1.

[1] The text from *K.A.R.*, 105, rev. 8-9, supplemented from *K.A.R.* 361. Ebeling has treated the text in *M.V.A.G.*, 1918, pp. 25 f.

[2] Cf. the translation of Ebeling in *A.O.T.*, 2nd ed., pp. 247-8. Ferris J. Stephens translates (in Pritchard, *A.N.E.T.*, 1950, p. 387): 'Whosoever shall learn this text (and) glorify the judge of the gods, may Shamash enrich his ..., may he make pleasing his command of the people.'

[3] The text is from René Labat with his emendations; cf. *Le poème babylonien de la Création*, 1935, pp. 172 f.

Turning to West-Semitic culture we remark that it is quite apparent that the written word is not valued highly. It is not considered an independent mode of expression. Even if the Qurân has given rise to a 'theology of Scripture' which may well be comparable with that of Judaism and Protestantism, the written copies of the Qurân play an astonishingly unobtrusive role in Islam. The Qurân has constantly—as in the first days of its existence—been handed down orally; everyone who wants to be admitted to the mosque of Al-Azhar (in Cairo) must be able to recite the whole Qurân without hesitation, and their holy writ is learned by heart by one of the initiated reciting it and the younger disciples repeating it until they know it by heart.[1]

The role of tradition in the culture of Islam is moreover so well-known that it is unnecessary to waste more words on the subject. (To guard against an overestimation of oral tradition in this field the reader is referred to the already mentioned work of Widengren.) Still, it is of importance to state that though the Arabs have great esteem for the spoken word, this is in no way peculiar to the Arabs. On the contrary, in that respect Islam is at one with antiquity, in the Semitic as well as the non-Semitic world. Beside the above quotations from Accadian texts, we may refer to the Old Testament, to Judaism—and in this connection we may mention primitive Christianity —and furthermore to sporadic features in the history of the Syrian Church, and likewise to the conditions under which tradition arose in the ancient Indian, Persian, and Greek cultures.[2] Especially interesting are the conditions in Judaism. We quote one illustration, easily accessible to the reader in Dalman's *Aramäische Dialektproblem*, 2nd ed., 1927, pp. 19 f.[3] The story tells of Johanan ben Zakkai in the camp of Vespasian.

---

[1] On this, cf. Johs. Pedersen, *Den arabiske Bog*, 1946, pp. 1-15

[2] As to India, cf. F. Max Müller, 'Literature before Letters', in *Last Essays*, 1st series, pp. 110-138, 1901; as to Persia, cf. H. S. Nyberg, *Irans forntida Religioner*, 1937, pp. 7 f, 451-478, F. Nau in *R.H.R.*, xcv, 1927, pp. 149-199; as to Greece, cf. W. Schmied, *Geschichte d. griech. Lit.*, I, i, 1927, pp. 19 f; as to Judaism, cf. Juda Bergman, 'Das Judentum in der hellenistisch-römischen Zeit', pp. 27-42, and esp. Michael Guttmann, 'Zur Entstehung des Talmuds', pp. 43 60, both from *Entwicklungsstufen d. jüd. Religion*, 1927; as to the Syrian Church, cf. *Revue de l'Orient Chrétien*, 2nd ser. ii, pp. 383 f

[3] From Midrash Echa, i, 31

After he had been received in audience by Vespasian for the first time, 'they seized him and locked him up with seven locks, and asked him what time it was at night, and he told them, (and) what time it was during the day, and he told them. And how did our master Johanan ben Zakkai know? From his recitation of the Mishnah.' In other words Rabbi Johanan ben Zakkai not only knew his Mishnah by heart, but he knew just how long it took to recite each paragraph, and how much time he needed to get through it all.

As an explicit reaction against the spread of the art of writing we may cite the following words of Plato (from the *Phaedrus*). They are remarkable as a reaction which does not originate with the common people, the ignorant crude masses—illiterate people are not characterized by contempt, but by respect for the written word. These words represent rather an attitude Plato had in common with the intellectual aristocracy of his day.[1]

> Socrates: I heard, then, that at Naucratis, in Egypt, was one of the ancient gods of that country, the one whose sacred bird is called the ibis, and the name of the god himself was Theuth. He it was who invented numbers and arithmetic and geometry and astronomy, also draughts and dice, and, most important of all, letters. Now the king of all Egypt at that time was the god Thamus, who lived in the great city of the upper region, which the Greeks call the Egyptian Thebes, and they call the god himself Ammon. To him came Theuth to show his inventions, saying that they ought to be imparted to the other Egyptians. But Thamus asked what use there was in each, and as Theuth enumerated their uses, expressed praise or blame, according as he approved or disapproved. The story goes that Thamus said many things to Theuth in praise or blame of the various arts, which it would take too long to repeat; but when they came to the letters, 'This invention, O king,' said Theuth, 'will make the Egyptians wiser and will improve their memories; for it is an elixir of memory and wisdom that I have dis-

[1] E. Tr. by H. N. Fowler in Loeb Classical Library, *Plato*, i, pp. 560 f, 274C-275A (quoted by permission of the Editors)

covered'. But Thamus replied, 'Most ingenious Theuth, one man has the ability to beget arts, but the ability to judge of their usefulness or harmfulness to their users belongs to another; and now you, who are the father of letters, have been led by your affection to ascribe to them a power the opposite of that which they really possess. For this invention will produce forgetfulness in the minds of those who learn to use it, because they will not practise their memory. Their trust in writing, produced by external characters which are no part of themselves, will discourage the use of their own memory within them. You have invented an elixir not of memory, but of reminding; and you offer your pupils the appearance of wisdom, not true wisdom, for they will read many things without instruction and will therefore seem to know many things, when they are for the most part ignorant and hard to get along with, since they are not wise, but only appear wise.'

These words of Plato may stand as a marginal note to the panegyrical estimate in modern research of the significance of writing for the development of human culture. It is one thing that the use of writing opens the doors to the ancient culture *for us*. Quite another matter is the use and the evaluation of writing in the ancient cultures themselves.

(*b*) As suggested above, the modern estimate of tradition is dependent on its place in the cultural life. It has often been maintained, that this connection is of an organic character, in the proper sense of the word. Our memory is daily enervated by newspapers and libraries. To quote Max Müller:[1] 'Every day we seem to be piling heaps of ashes on the divine light within us. Men who read *The Times* every morning . . . or it may be serious works on such different subjects as geology, philology, geography or history are systematically ruining their memories. They are under the suzerainty of books and helpless without them . . . ' Therefore we inevitably listen with scepticism to information about the art of memory in antiquity. Surely, we should not have given much credit to Max Müller

[1] *Op. cit.*, p. 134

himself, had he not been so great a scientific authority, when he relates that thousands of Brahmins still learn the Rigveda by heart (153,826 words!), or when he tells of a blind Veda-student who in the course of twelve to thirteen years of study had brought matters to such a pass that he could be examined by means of Max Müller's printed text edition, and was always found accurate.[1] Although the Hindus have made use of writing since the fifth or fourth century B.C., they have retained oral tradition. Why? Cult and religion are always rather immune to technical improvements, are always wedded to tradition. The Vedas were a divine message, handed down orally from one generation to the other, without the aid of writing; therefore the oral tradition is continued into the age of writing.[2]

We now propound the question, In what fields was oral tradition active in antiquity? And to what extent, in what *milieu*, for what purpose was *writing* used? What technical means were employed to master tradition? In the nature of things, it is comparatively easier to bring to light authentic testimonies to the role of written transmission than to the role of oral tradition. This fact, however, ought not to discourage scholars from making an *attempt* to arrive at a plausible statement of the circumstances in which tradition thrived in antiquity; but one is obliged to stress the hypothetical nature of the exposition when we are left entirely to conjecture.

A demarcation of the field of writing has already been outlined by H. S. Nyberg,[3] chiefly concerning pre-exilic Israel. 'Of course writing was used in pre-exilic Palestine, but it is doubtful whether it was used for purely literary purposes to any great extent. Writing was principally employed in practical matters, for contracts, covenants, monuments—in these cases doubtless also with magical significance—probably also for official registers and lists, and, above all, for letters. Annals were modelled on the Assyrian annals; legal texts of major importance were possibly committed to writing also. But the actual tradition of history, the epic tales, the cult-legends, doubtless generally the laws too, must in the main have been handed down orally. Writers should certainly not be reckoned

[1] *Op. cit.*, pp. 123, 130   [2] Ibid.   [3] *Studien zum Hoseabuche*, pp. 7 f

24

among the prophets and poets except with the greatest caution. The art of writing was the business of the specialist, not of the common man, as it always has been in the Orient.' We can acknowledge the validity of these words with reference to the Old Testament with but few reservations. To a lesser or greater degree they apply to the related cultures too, and to the communities on the same level of culture as ancient Israel.

Let us begin with the last point: the art of writing is the business of the specialist and not of the common man. This thesis is fully confirmed by the ancient Egyptian literature. Certainly stories and songs have been preserved from Old Egypt which are characterized by their popular form and their appeal to popular taste, permeated by popular naïveté. Adolf Erman[1] maintains that this literary genre originates from story-tellers who then walked about in the streets of the great cities and gathered the crowds by their narrative art even as they do to-day. But the major part of the Egyptian literature, as it has been handed down, is explicitly aristocratic in spirit, and is known for its elegance of language and style. The reason is that the men who were responsible for that kind of literature were the writers, the clerks, who were in the service of kings and sanctuaries and who were recruited from the highest class of the population. Erman mentions[2] a group of 'school-writings' that praise the lot of the clerks at the expense of other classes of society. Naturally these writings have their special purpose: to spur on the clerks by exaggerating their good fortune. However, there is without doubt some sort of truth in the following:[3] 'Do not become an officer, a priest or a baker. Become a clerk. He is released from labour, protected against work; he is free from hoeing with the hoe, and you need not carry any knife.' The officer runs the risk of lying prostrate before his superiors and exposing himself to the danger of losing his life; the priests may be compelled to do public service; the baker runs the risk of falling into the oven and so perishing in the flames; but the clerk, he is fortunate: 'He directs all that is done in this country.'

No one who has been initiated a little into the mysteries of

---

[1] *Literatur der Ägypter*, pp. 8 f   [2] *Op. cit.*, pp. 242 f   [3] Ibid., pp. 250 f

cuneiform writing will deny that the noble art of writing in Mesopotamian culture was an art belonging to the specialist —at any rate not to the man in the street. The following text,[1] consisting of a dialogue between teacher and pupil, may be quoted:[2]

The teacher:

2 ina pu-ḫur [u] m-ma-ni ki-sal [É DUB-pi e?-rib?]

Into the congregation of the learned, into the court of the [tablet-house step in]

3 al-ka ma-ri ti-šab ina pa [-ni-ia]

Come, my son, sit down befo[re me]

4 ga-na lu-uq-bi-kúm-ma pi-te [uz-na-ka]

See, I will speak to you, and open [your ear!]

5 ul-tu UD-um ṣe-ḫe-ri-ka a-di be-lu-t[i-ka]

From the day of your childhood until that of [your] manhood

6 ina É DUB-pi a[š?-ba?-ta?]

do you [sit] in the tablet-house;

7 DUB.SAR-ru-ta ta-ḫu-zu i-da-as-sa ul t[i-di]

the art of writing on tablets which you learn, its signs you do not know.

---

[1] The major part of the text is from *K.A.R.* 111, but is unfortunately of a very fragmentary nature, especially towards the end. It may be supplemented from *K.A.R.* 367. The transcription is by J. Læssøe. The italicized portions are supplied from 367.

[2] On the whole question of schools and the art of writing, cf. also L. Dürr, *Das Erziehungswesen im Alten Testament und im Antiken Orient* (M.V.A.G., xxxvi, No. 2), 1932, and now also G. R. Driver, *Semitic Writing*, (Schweich Lectures for 1944), 1948, pp. 62-73: 'Scholars and Scribes', from which we note the following statements:

(1) that the knowledge of the signs among the Sumerians and Accadians was generally 'the peculiar possession of a professional class of clerks or scribes', was even called a 'secret treasure' or 'mystery', although it was often the case that 'a fair number of laymen could read if not write the cuneiform script' (p. 62), which was true of Ashurbanipal for instance, (p. 72). (In a study on 'Literacy and Oral Tradition' in *Festskrift til Johs. Pedersen*, 1953, J. Læssøe gives some instances of this.)

(2) that the tablet-writer school, 'bīt ṭuppātē', Sum. : E.DUB.BA, was often attached to the big temples.

The text discussed below is also discussed (p. 65f.) by Driver, who however only uses *K.A.R.* 111. His reading 'qi-*na*-am-ma' (l. 12) must be rejected in favour of qi-ba-am-ma; cf. the connection. Line 15 which reads thus: '[r]e-eš SAR.-ru-ti sa-an-tak-ku iš . . .' = 'the art of writing is the first of the kingdom' reflects according to Driver (p.72) the popular attitude towards the art of writing as a craft that led to the highest posts in the state. Læssøe supplies '[r]e-eš [DUB] SAR.-ru-ti' 'the first of the art of writing'—a reading worth consideration.

		The scholar:
8	me-nu-ú šá la i-du-u	What is there that I do not know?
		The teacher:
9	me-na-a ti-*di*	What do you know?
10	gán-na lu-šal-ka-ma *qí-ba-a*	See, I will question you, and you shall speak.
11	gán-na lu-uq-bi-kam-ma ap-la-*an-ni*	See, I will speak, and you shall answer me.
		The scholar:
12	šá-la-an-ni-ma lu-uq-bi-ka qí-ba-am-ma *lu-pu-ul-ka*	Question me and I will tell you; speak to me and I will answer you.
		The teacher:
13	ul tap-pal-*an-ni*	You (can)not answer me.
		The scholar:
14	[a]m-me-ni la *ap-pal-ka*	Why should I not (be able to) answer you?

The rest is too fragmentary to permit an understanding of the text. Line 15 is presumably a sentence uttered by the scholar. Lines 16, 18, and 20 end in 'ti-di-e', and are thus probably questions asked by the teacher; from this one may conclude that lines 17, 19, and 21 are the scholar's replies.[1]

The pupils in the writing-schools sat at the feet of the school-teacher and they acquired their knowledge through questions and answers. These specialists were indispensable to business-men and jurists, and the old imperialistic rulers very often made use of them not only to immortalize their deeds, but also to take care of the diplomatic correspondence. Their employment in practical affairs is proved by thousands of

[1] The dialogue is preserved bi-lingually. According to A. Falkenstein, 'Der "Sohn des Tafelhauses"', *Die Welt des Orients*, 1948, pp. 172-186, the dialogue is perhaps a late new edition of an older Sumerian didactic poem that has only been preserved in Sumerian. The important parts of it are translated and annotated in the same article. A more complete edition has been published by S. N. Kramer in *J.A.O.S.*, lxix, 1949, pp. 199-215: 'Schooldays.' Falkenstein concludes his article (pp. 185 f) by stressing the association between the schools and the cultural centre through the ages. Originally this was undoubtedly the temple, in the New-Sumerian period (Third dynasty of Ur) the king's court, later again the temple.

economic and judicial contracts. It is the specialists who draw up the tablets; the contracting parties roll their seals over them as signatures. The picture which thus presents itself for research is not that of inferior classes characterized by illiteracy in contrast to upper classes able to read and write, but a special guild of writers, of clerks in the service of the public, the princes, and the temples. In Egypt at any rate these clerks were recruited from the upper classes, but otherwise throughout the whole Orient they were educated and instructed, trained and taught in schools of writing. Very likely every school had its own traditions, which were, of course, handed down by word of mouth in the daily instruction (cf. *supra*).

Let us dwell a little on two points mentioned above, the clerks in the service of temples, and those in the service of princes, especially with regard to their diplomatic correspondence.

The fact that religious and epic texts of major importance in the high cultures of the Ancient Near East were ordinarily put into written form has already been stressed in the case of Egyptian literature. The evidence points in a similar direction in the case of Mesopotamian literature. But from a few Mesopotamian texts we gain the impression that *written* transmission was not so absolutely exclusive as to leave no room for oral tradition. The importance of learning the sacred texts by heart was stressed, and that may have had practical consequences. Certainly Widengren[1] maintains that the texts—which were perhaps often dictated, and possibly sometimes from memory —were nevertheless always written, and that this was the way in which they were transmitted; and further, that the practice of committing texts to memory was certainly in existence in Mesopotamian education, but that this tells us nothing about the real transmission of the texts, 'for these were handed down from one generation to the next in written form'. I have, however, one example which may introduce a minor correction. In a hymn to Ea, Shamash, Marduk, and Sin[2], we remark the following colophon: a-na [K]A UM.ME.A. [ša-ṭ]ir GAB! RI! la!-

---

[1] In his aforementioned work, p. 91 with note 1
[2] H. F. Lutz, *Selected Sumerian and Babylonian Texts*, 1919, No. 106

bi-ru ul a-mur, i.e. 'written from the scholar's dictation' (literally, after the mouth of the scholar, Sum. UM.ME.A = Accad. ummānu = scholar), 'the old edition I have not seen'. The expression 'ana pī' (Sum. KA = Accad. pū) corresponds exactly to the Hebrew 'mip-pī' of Jer. 36.4 and 18.

As to the second point, the diplomatic correspondence, it is generally recognized among students of the Ancient Near East that letters are composed in such a manner that they reflect an orally delivered message, no matter whether the message was orally delivered or not.[1] This holds good especially with regard to Accadian letters, but may also have been true of Old-Israelite letters. Certainly we have not any diplomatic documents preserved from pre-exilic Israel in the Old Testament literature, the wording of which might be adduced as proof. It appears, however, from several texts, that the normal method of diplomatic correspondence was for a delegation of men to deliver the message from their king orally with due homage, the king having provided them with letters as a means of control and perhaps as an aid to memory. II Kings 20.12 f is rather instructive: 'At that time Merodach-ben-Baladan, king of Babylon, sent *letters* and a gift to Hezekiah, for he had heard that Hezekiah had been ill. And Hezekiah *listened* to them, and he showed them his whole house,' etc.; and in v. 14: 'And the prophet Isaiah went to king Hezekiah, and he said to him: What have these men *said*, and from whence have they come to you?'

Such a passage is indeed a fine illustration of the form of address in Accadian letters. The formula is easily found in both of the archives which are of the highest importance to, and have direct bearing on, Old Testament study, the archives

---

[1] Cf. especially O. Schroeder, 'Briefe' in *Reallexikon der Assyriologie*, ii, 1938, pp. 62 f where it is stated that the introductory formulas of old Accadian letters reflect the fact that even before the invention of writing stereotyped phrases were in use when an oral message was delivered, and that when writing was invented, 'blieb dem Boten—auch als Träger eines Briefes—oft die Aufgabe, sich mündlich seiner Meldung zu entledigen: das Geschriebene selbst diente einmal zu seiner Beglaubigung, zum anderen auch wohl als Stütze des Gedächtnisses'. From the fact that some Old Babylonian tablets contained more than one letter—*V.A.S.*, xvi, No. 7 has for instance three—the following conclusion is drawn: 'Auch Tafeln, die mehrere Briefe vereinigen waren unmöglich zu Ablieferung bestimmt, sondern sollten dem Boten eine Merkhilfe für seine mündlichen Meldungen sein' (ibid.).

from Mari (Tell Ḥariri, eighteenth to seventeenth century B.C.) and El-Amarna (fourteenth century B.C.). From the latter[1] we may take the following, very typical, introductory formula:

a-na šarri[ri] beli-ia ᵈšamši-ia qi-bí-ma	To the king, my Lord, my Sun Speak:
um-ma Ri-ib-Addi ardu-ka-ma	So has spoken Rib-Addi, thy servant:
a-na šepe beli-ia ᵈšamši-ia	To the feet of my Lord, my Sun,
7-šu 7-ta-an am-ku-ut	I prostrate myself 7 times 7 [times].

and then the special contents of the letter follow. Still more interesting, however, are some formulae from letters from the Mari-archives. A very frequent one we may call (*a*): 'tuppakā ša tušābilam ešmē', i.e. your tablet which you did send forth, I have heard;[2] another we may call (*b*):[3] 'šimēšu' = hear it, that is acquaint yourself with the contents of a letter I have sent,[4] or an optative 'lišmēšu' = may he hear it.[5]

From this little *excursus* we return to the consideration of written and oral tradition. From the above quotations from Egyptian literature it might be tempting to conclude that written literature belonged to aristocratic circles, that it was superior to the popular level, whereas oral tradition was popular tradition, and the possession of everyone. The question is, however, not quite so simple. In a sense oral tradition really belongs to the people, because the people are the ones that listen, and as listeners they strengthen the oral tradition; they are an important element of control. But the active preservation of tradition does not simply belong to everybody. The bearers and creators of tradition are—no less than the bearers of written transmission—specialists, whether narrators or rhapsodists, or saga-tellers, or singers and poets, or reciters of

---

[1] Knudtzon, *Die El-Amarna-Tafeln*, (V.A.B., II, i), 1915, pp. 460 ff, No. 104
[2] Cf. *Archives Royales de Mari*, i, 6,5; 9,5; 10,4; 20,5; 22,4; 37,5; 47,4,8; etc.
[3] A third formula (*c*) reads thus: 'tuppi annām ina šemēm', literally, by the hearing of this tablet, cf. i, 14,13; 31,33; etc.
[4] Cf. i, 16,8; 24,5; etc.
[5] i, 49,15; 52,7

law. And the types of literature with which *these* specialists deal are not only popular stories and fairy-tales, to which children and grown-ups listen with enthusiasm 'on leisurely winter evenings', but also literature as aristocratic and artificial as one could wish. Probably nobody would venture to call the Homeric epics popular; on the contrary they are aristocratic, both in structure and as to content. It is the nobility that is glorified, and the singers are the professional bards, who at the banquets held at the courts of the nobility bring out their clear-sounding lyres and celebrate the renown of the men in songs that resound to high heaven, tales of Ulysses and the Peleid Achilles.[1] And the Homeric epics seem to have been created in the oral tradition, without the aid of writing; for some centuries they were handed down by word of mouth exclusively. Now it is interesting that the fact that they were put into writing did not at all put an end to the oral recitation or transmission of them. A whole guild of 'rhapsodists' appeared—especially at the festivals—as reciters of Homer, giving recitations of all the songs.[2]

From Xenophon's *Symposium* III, 5*b* we learn that the recitation from memory (ἀπὸ στόματος εἰπεῖν) was nothing exceptional, and not limited to the circle of the rhapsodists. Moreover, it is well worth mentioning that written copies of the Homeric epics were preserved in the temples from an early date as a means of regulating the text and as an aid to the rhapsodists in their recitation.

So far we have been concerned with rhythmical poems, where the structure may have been of the greatest value as an

[1] Cf. Od. IX, 55 f
[2] As this guild grew in importance such rhapsodists might have an audience of several thousand people; cf. Plato's dialogue, *Ion*. With the above quotation from the *Phaedrus* in mind, it may perhaps seem a little odd that Plato in the *Ion* does not think very highly of those who excel in the difficult art of memory; he says contemptuously of them that they have no systematic knowledge whatever of that which they recite, and that their activity is regulated by business motives. There need not, however, be any contradiction between the view expressed in the *Phaedrus*, and Plato's opinion of the rhapsodists as we find it in the *Ion*. An objection to a purely mechanical memorization does not in itself mean that one anathematizes all oral transmission. Contempt for mere external memorization was probably common to the whole circle around Socrates, for in Xenophon's works (*Symposium* III, 5*b*; *Memorabilia* IV, ii, 10) these rhapsodists are called 'very foolish'; no class is ἠλιθιώτερον ῥαψῳδῶν.

Old Iceland?

aid to memory. But what about prose? It will be sufficient here to draw attention to the technique of saga-composition and saga-tradition in Old Iceland, a type of literature that may —just like Homer—be deemed aristocratic in form and content, and here too specialists were in charge of the tradition. We will restrict ourselves to quoting an episode to which Rudolf Meissner, a German scholar, has called attention in his book, *Die Strengleikar*.[1] The episode is from 'Morkinskinna', 72.18: the king Harald Haarderaade was once sought out by a man from Iceland who came to ask for maintenance. When the king asked him if he was a master of any craft, he replied that he knew how to tell sagas. This resulted in his being engaged. It was summer when the Icelander came to the king, and his repertoire was expected to last till Christmas—that was at any rate the king's estimate. However, during the Christmas celebrations for thirteen successive evenings he recited one continuous saga describing the king's expedition to Russia and the Mediterranean, a saga abounding in battles and adventures. He gave detailed information about the origin of the saga: he worked it out little by little on the basis of a narrative by an eye-witness.[2]

(*c-d*) In this connection it would be natural to mention the possibility of interplay between written and oral tradition. Regarding the Homeric epics we have just pointed out two methods of tradition running side by side: the public recitation of the poems by a whole guild of masters of tradition and reciters, and the written copies deposited in different places as a means of control for, and aid to, oral recitation. A similar interplay existed in Ancient Mesopotamia, and we have at least one distinct parallel in the Old Testament; cf. the 'introduction' in Deut. 31 to the song of Moses.

If we suppose that tradition was once almost exclusively oral, then we must proceed to propound the question: Why have traditionists, poets and reciters made use of writing, and what consequences does this involve? These questions are

---

[1] *Op. cit.*, 1902, p. 88
[2] Anyone wishing for further information about the traditions behind the Icelandic family sagas is referred to Knut Liestöl's *Upphavet til den islandske ættesaga*, 1929

of course not only of interest for the Homeric poems; they must be asked regarding every culture or cultural movement whatsoever, where the spoken—proclaimed—word was of primary significance, but where at some specified time writing nevertheless came into use. Thus these questions must be of the greatest interest to those concerned with Biblical research. It is certainly difficult, if not impossible, to give an answer that applies equally to the Old Nordic, the Hellenic, the Persian, the Indian, and the Semitic worlds. Especially in those cases where there was interplay between several civilizations, the answer must have many different nuances. But it is perhaps possible to indicate an incentive that at certain times made people start to write down their inherited traditions. Here we would draw attention to the answer of Engnell and Nyberg[1] that 'reduction to writing is linked with a general crisis of confidence'. At some time faith in the spoken word began to waver, and it was thought necessary to write down the traditions.

Many different impulses are of importance here, such as influence from neighbouring cultures, the menace of political disintegration, the dying out of the traditionists, the wish for safeguards as secure as possible in periods of cultural fusion, etc.[2]

What consequences does a reduction to writing involve? What really happens when one makes use of writing? It has too often been asserted from an insufficient knowledge of the oral practice within ancient cultures that the reduction to writing involves the first literary (in the true sense of the word) treatment of the traditions, the editing and grouping of a formless mass of tradition. What has been said above should have shown that this theory is untenable. Far nearer to the truth are those who claim that a reduction to writing means in the main only that a tradition in a more or less fortuitous form is fixed on paper.[3] And yet something new has happened. It is

[1] Cf. Engnell, *Gamla Testamentet*, p. 42
[2] Several of these motives have undoubtedly had a hand in the creation of the Old Testament as well as the New Testament canons
[3] This view was maintained already by Rudolf Meissner regarding the Old Icelandic sagas (*Die Strengleikar*, 1902, p. 104)

not only a purely technical matter, the inauguration of a different method of transmission, which clearly shows its departure from the usual one by the appearance of a series of different text-variants, but an impersonal intermediary link has been introduced between the bearer of tradition and the receiver. Where the oral form of education was the predominant one, and where great emphasis was laid on the personal contact between teacher and pupil,[1] this inanimate intermediary link in a living tradition can hardly have had immediate consequences of any importance. But if one imagines the living chain of tradition weakened, even cut off, so that only the documents are left, then the interpretation first and foremost becomes a problem, when the tradition is to be resurrected. Prose and poetry that has achieved a stable, concise mode of expression, either from the very beginning from the hand of the master or from generations of traditionists, falls into the hands of novices. In the most favourable circumstances these will be uncertain as to a whole series of details in the texts; in the least favourable they will force their own interpretation on the material and, as they say, 'arrange' the text.[2]

We have above indicated two types of interplay between written and oral tradition: a writing down of the tradition while it is still flourishing, so that the two methods of trans-

---

Cf. for Islam Johs. Pedersen, *Den arabiske Bog*, 1946, pp. 14 and 18 f

[2] The excerpt from Plato's *Phaedrus* quoted above continues with some reflections of Socrates which may well be mentioned in this connection. (275D f) Writing is compared to painting, the figures of which certainly resemble living beings, but are dumb. If one asks the letters, they can only say one thing, and 'every word, when once it is written, is bandied about, alike among those who understand and those who have no interest in it, and it knows not to whom to speak or not to speak; when ill-treated or unjustly reviled it always needs its father to help it; *for it has no power to protect or help itself*' (αὐτὸς γὰρ οὔτ' ἀμύνασθαι οὔτε βοηθῆσαι δυνατὸς αὑτῷ). Finally the use of writing is compared to the Adonis-gardens, the pleasure-gardens, which are sown in the heat of summer, and where the plants shoot up rapidly but die before they put forth fruit. The wise man will always choose suitable soil 'and be pleased when those which he had sowed reached their perfection in the eighth month', and in the same way the man who has knowledge of the right, the beautiful, and the good will renounce the use of pen and ink, of words 'which cannot defend themselves by argument and cannot teach the truth effectually' (ἀδυνάτων δὲ ἱκανῶς τἀληθῆ διδάξαι). He will *only* use the Adonis-garden, 'the gardens of letters', 'to treasure up reminders for himself, when he comes to the forgetfulness of old age, and for others who follow the same path, and he will be pleased when he sees them putting forth tender leaves'.

mission run side by side, possibly so that the written one represents an aid or support of the oral one; or—a possibility
which must remain theoretical for the present—one long chain
of tradition stretching through many generations with one or
more links that have been entirely of a written nature, so that
the oral tradition has been broken off for shorter or longer
periods. Kn. Liestöl has touched on the second possibility[1] of
interplay between written and oral tradition with regard to
the Icelandic family sagas. He suggests that incidents from
the sagas may have been written down so that one could use
these notes for reading aloud or as an aid to oral delivery, and
that later saga-writers could borrow either from such rough
copies or from the oral delivery of them, and weave historically
irrelevant episodes into their own sagas wherever they could
fit them in. If there were such written intermediate links more
details might perhaps be preserved than by a wholly oral
transmission. But only perhaps. In spite of everything one
still has to reckon with narrators and listeners who could
remember a wealth of detail; one has to assume a practised and
highly developed narrative art; and Liestöl admits plainly that
as far as the Icelandic sagas are concerned there is no special
reason for supposing that tradition passed through a written
stage. Even though an interplay of this nature between the
two methods of transmission may not have taken place in Iceland, it is still both possible and probable that it did take place
in other countries, and it ought to be considered whether such
an interplay might not cast light upon the extraordinary literary
riddles presented by the literature of antiquity, and among
these the Old Testament's treasure of *epos*. For instance, when
we come across heterogeneous matter[2] in the epic material in
Genesis, (we might here mention Gen. 10, 14, 34, 36, 38, material which has, however, now been merged with the other
material by the author(s), perhaps even in a more organic way
than is generally assumed in literary-critical circles), we might
be tempted to ask, whether written traditions did not exist in

[1] *Op. cit.*, ch. II
[2] 'Matter that cannot be fitted into the sources', cf. Bentzen, *Indledning*, 1941,
p. 62, or 'Material outside the Strata' in Bentzen, *Introduction*, 2nd ed., ii, 1952,
pp. 59 f, where especially Gen. 14 is discussed

these special cases, at any rate at that period when they were introduced into the great mass of traditions. It does not, however, follow necessarily that the author(s) actually worked with written sources in these cases; these separate traditions might have been worked in at some time before the final writing of the work.

Finally we may briefly touch on the question of possible criteria of oral or written tradition. It would seem that one has to reckon with two categories. If we have only a single account, a prose narrative for instance, it is possible to decide from certain formal criteria with a reasonable degree of probability whether it may have been handed down orally. The formal characteristics here are: a monotonous style, recurrent expressions, a fluent, paratactic style, a certain rhythm and euphony which are especially noticeable when one hears the account, and finally anacolutha which a literary writer would hardly have let pass, but which may have been accompanied by a gesture in oral delivery or even have come into existence by the incorporation of a 'stage direction' in the text.[1] To this may be added most of the epic laws formulated by A. Olrik and others, especially the 'law of repetition', and the 'law of the number three', and 'the scenic law of the number two'. A conscious emphasizing of 'memory words' and 'representative themes' may also betray an organic connection with oral tradition and composition.

This category of criteria is evidently most useful for prose texts, and it may be used when we have only a single text to work with.

In the case of double accounts, whether both are dependent on an earlier written or oral stratum, or one of them is dependent on the other, we have—if there are discrepancies between the accounts or the songs—another category of criteria that may be used with greater certainty. It is in short a question of the study of written and oral variation. Here we follow Liestøl,[2] who distinguishes the following characteristics for written variation: errors of the copyist, words *read* wrong, or interchanged, sentences omitted through dittography or haplo-

rather arbitrary

---

[1] A well-known instance is Mark 2.10*b*, and parallels   [2] *Op. cit.*, p. 38

graphy, words in the text revised. If a larger or smaller passage has been lost, it is supplied from memory, or interpolations are made from other sources at the disposal of the copyist.

Oral tradition is indicated by variants produced by errors in hearing, or the confusion of words that *sound* alike. Whole episodes are forgotten. Or they are added by the traditionist from memory, but possibly in the wrong place. On the whole the separate episodes change places more easily, especially when they can just as well be in one place as another.

It is thus evident that it is not the greater or lesser similarity as such that determines whether it is a question of written or oral tradition, but the kind of similarity, graphic or phonetic.

Lastly as to the problem of the reliability of oral tradition, it must be strongly emphasized that one would be much mistaken in asserting that the oral tradition was subject to no control. Especially in those cases where tradition is flourishing, i.e. where there are many traditionists of the same text, the individual traditionist has a very small chance of carrying through a corrupt recension. His guild brothers, but first of all his listeners, have been of immeasurable importance in upholding the tradition, whether these listeners were teachers who were to examine the scholars in the canonical texts (cf. late Judaism, Parseeism, Islam), private members of the tribe who heard the exploits of their tribe celebrated in the odes of the tribal poets (as the Bedouin do to this day),[1] or those taking part in the annual national and religious festivals (e.g. Israel). Bound to its own *milieu*, to the rhythm of the day and the year, the spoken word is heard in the situation intended for it; it is not dependent on 'external, foreign $\tau \acute{\upsilon} \pi o\iota$' and thus does not run the risk of creating '$\delta o \xi \acute{o} \sigma o \phi o\iota - \grave{a} \nu \tau \grave{\iota} \ \sigma o \phi \hat{\omega} \nu$'.

It may seem that I tend to consider the appearance of writing in tradition as a sign of cultural degeneration.[2] I willingly

---

[1] Cf. Musil, *Arabia Petræa*, iii, 1908, p. 233

[2] Similar points of view have been advanced by the late Professor Causse in his valuable work *Les plus vieux chants de la Bible*, 1926, esp. p. 141, n. 2: 'Cette fixation de la parole traditionelle par l'écriture devait avoir les conséquences les plus considérables pour l'avenir. Mais au moment où elle a commencé elle n'avait qu'une importance secondaire et toute de conservation. A un certain point de vue elle marquait une décadence, car, elle devait suppléer au manque de spontanéité et de ténacité de la tradition orale', and according to Causse, this

admit my debt to Plato in this respect, but at the same time I would emphasize that degeneration is better than eternal obliteration, or, if not better, at least more useful to research in later times. Thanks to this degeneration we are now able, with a reasonable degree of probability, to give an opinion as to the form and contents of texts of the particular traditionist(s) who are the real authors of the written recension we have before us. It is of importance to the Biblical scholar that he should realize this. If we should be so fortunate as to be able to determine that a manuscript was written at such and such a time, either by means of appended colophons or by purely technical means, the question arises whether this is the 'official' recension of the time in question (if it had any such), or whether we have come across an apocryphal, perhaps sectarian, recension. This question must for instance be taken into consideration in the debate about the manuscripts found in the cave by the Dead Sea, when one wishes to determine the significance of these manuscripts for the Massoretic text of Isaiah or Habakkuk. Only when one has taken these considerations into account can he start on the still more complicated way back through a possible oral tradition—often a question of generations, perhaps even centuries. Here we have to use everything we can collect concerning the technique of oral composition and tradition (the forming of collections, the catchword principle, mnenotechnics, sources of errors in oral transmission), and combine this with considerations as to genuineness and integrity, and with analyses of the author's time—analyses where the emphasis is placed on contemporaneous sources, where such are to be had, especially inscriptions and purely archaeological data which tell us about the economic and cultural conditions of that time. But where our specimens of literature can naturally be fitted into such an analysis, we have no right and no reason to doubt the reliability of tradition, and this holds good, even though our preconceived hypotheses, whatever they are, cannot be confirmed, or perhaps even have to be rejected, in face of the evidence of tradition.

'manque de spontanéité et de ténacité de la tradition orale' is due to the political and social crises which followed the establishment of the kingdom, p. 141.

III

THE ROLE OF ORAL TRADITION
IN THE OLD TESTAMENT

THE point of departure for this chapter is taken from Nyberg's words: 'The written Old Testament is a creation of the post-exilic Jewish community; of what existed earlier undoubtedly only a small part was in fixed written form.'[1] That is to say, the Old Testament as *written* literature may in all probability be ascribed to the period between the destruction of Jerusalem in 587 B.C. and the time of the Maccabees.

In what follows we shall attempt to demonstrate the tenability of this thesis, firstly, in a negative manner, by establishing the subordinate role of writing in pre-exilic Israel; secondly, in a positive manner, by tracing the more direct evidence of oral transmission in the Old Testament itself; and finally, we shall briefly touch on the problem how a written canon can come into existence in an age that demonstrably still venerates the spoken word.

Let us begin with a few fundamental remarks. The principal source of our knowledge of pre-exilic Israelite culture is the Old Testament itself. Those who maintain the generally recognised conception of the unreliability of oral tradition will deny that anyone taking Nyberg's thesis of the origin of the written Old Testament in post-exilic times seriously has the right to say anything of importance about the pre-exilic culture on the basis of the Old Testament itself—always excepting that which in the Old Testament itself is expressly indicated as being taken from written sources, 'the Book of Songs', 'the Book of the Upright', 'the Book of the Wars of YHWH' and above all that which must be presumed to originate from the Israelite and Judahite annals.

In the previous chapter we attempted to create a new attitude to tradition, a favourable one, characterized by faith in the

[1] *Studien zum Hoseabuche*, 1935, p. 8

reliability of this method of transmission, or at least in its possibilities in this respect. Not only was there a different technical mastery of tradition from any that exists in our culture; the desire to disregard tradition was also absent. The individual's sovereignty over the material handed down from his fathers was foreign to the ancients. On the basis of Old Testament literature we can therefore hopefully begin to point out where and when writing was used in pre-exilic Israel, and where and when the spoken word was employed.

Naturally we are obliged to consult modern Palestinian archaeology to see if it can supplement, or merely confirm, or even perhaps revise, our conception of the culture of ancient Israel in this respect.

1. Statistics of the occurrence of words such as 'kāthabh', 'sēpher', etc., demonstrate as clearly as could be wished that the use of writing for really literary purposes belongs essentially to the exilic and post-exilic times. But at the same time such statistics show that writing was used to a considerable extent for more practical purposes, and if the Old Testament had not been a collection of texts chosen from a religious standpoint, but more especially composed of political, juridical, profane, poetical, mercantile, and grammatical elements, the statistics would certainly show a still more widespread use of writing in pre-exilic Israel than is now the case.

In the Tetrateuch we find that there is no testimony to the use of writing either in Genesis or in Leviticus. In Leviticus, which does not really contain narrative portions, there is perhaps not so much reason to expect any reference to the use of writing. As to Genesis, the Jewish commentator B. Jacob has drawn attention to the fact that it is more likely a literary fiction than a true tradition, that the use of writing was unknown in pre-Mosaic times, a fiction which it was not possible to carry through entirely; cf. the term 'sēpher tōledhōth' (Gen. 5.1), and the mention of Judah's signet (Gen. 38.18).[1] The fiction becomes apparent in Gen. 23.1-19, Abraham's purchase of the field with the cave of Machpelah At this 'oral' stage of Israelite culture *no* document is drawn up, although the business

[1] *Genesis*, 1934, p. 320

world was the largest employer of clerks then as it is now.[1]

In Exodus we come across the verb 'kāthabh' eleven times, nine of them in Ex. 24 and 32-34, referring to the tablets of stone with the Decalogue, and one of them, Ex. 24.4, to the book of the Covenant. The two remaining instances are Ex. 39.30, which mentions the inscription 'Holy to JHWH' on the frontlet of the High Priest, and Ex. 17.14—the only place in the Tetrateuch that mentions a really *literary* activity of Moses— the recording in a document of the victory over the Amalekites. In Numbers, evidence of writing is given five times: in the mention of Aaron's blossoming rod, Num. 17.17 f (the use of writing as a mark of ownership); the station catalogue, Num. 33.2; Num. 11.26, which states that the names of the seventy elders were written down; and Num. 5.23, where the letters seem to possess a supernatural power, in the text which provides for the ordeal for a woman suspected of unfaithfulness, Num. 5.11-31. Finally we must mention Num. 21.14, which speaks of a 'sēpher milḥamōth JHWH', a passage we shall return to later.

As to Deuteronomy and the Deuteronomistic history the matter stands thus, that the use of writing (from a statistical point of view) is concentrated on (*a*) 'this Book of the Law', 'the Book of the Law of Moses', 'the Book of this Covenant' (the last expression from II Kings 23.21), and (*b*) the annals, which are mentioned for the first time towards the end of the account of Solomon, I Kings 11.41, and for the last time regarding the northern kingdom, II Kings 15.31 (Pekah b. Remaliah), and regarding the kingdom of Judah, II Kings 24.5 (Jehoiakim). The formula with which the Deuteronomist refers

---

[1] In Accadian culture it was the rule that only the agreement that was fixed in writing was juridically valid. Cf. O. Weber, *Die Literatur der Babylonier und Assyrer*, 1907, p. 249. A comparison between Gen. 23 and Jer. 32 forces itself upon us. Jeremiah has to have a written contract drawn up and has to conclude the bargain before witnesses, which again goes to show that the written word evidently did not have the same independent position that it has in our culture. With this one might compare, for instance, Codex Hammurabi §§ 122-124, which deal with the depositing of movables in the care of a fellow citizen. This must be done before witnesses and with a written contract, but the fact that the witnesses are the main point, psychologically speaking, is evident, since they are named first and the contract is not mentioned at all in § 124 (though naturally implied). The juridical contracts of daily life were furnished with the seals and (or) names of the witnesses.

to these annals is usually: 'Now the rest of the history of X., and all that he did, is it not written in the book of the Chronicles of the kings of Judah (Israel)?'

Even though we may surmise that written law-codices were very well known in pre-exilic Israel,[1] we refrain from treating group (a) as pre-exilic material. The question of the transmission of the laws will be dealt with in connection with Josh. 24.25 f and I Sam. 10.25.

As to the annals, the most divergent views have been expressed in the course of time. At one end we have Hölscher with his conception of the book of the Chronicles of the Kings of Judah, or Israel, as one great epic work continuing the Pentateuch, or rather those parts of the Pentateuch which are separated as the source 'E' and are supposed to have been composed sometime after 586 B.C.[2] At the other end stand Eissfeldt and Noth with the view that it is a question of semi-official or private publications, published after the deaths of the kings in question, since two things are apparently presupposed by the Deuteronomist: 1. that anyone who desires to do so can read more in the works referred to; and 2. that the reign of each king is presented as a completed whole, a fact that is not at all characteristic of annals which are added to year by year.[3] It is, however, questionable whether these conclusions can be drawn from the well-known quotation formula. It may merely be that the Deuteronomist wished to provide his work with a stamp of guarantee, and hence informs us that he has made use of the best sources, and that he has chosen the material which in his opinion was of essential importance. It would seem that the only necessary supposition is that the annals—both those of the Northern Kingdom and those of Judah—in some way survived the downfall of the kingdoms. The fact that Pekah and Jehoiakim are the last

---

[1] Hos. 8.12: 'Though I wrote my commands by the myriad for him, they were counted as a strange thing'; Isa. 10.1: 'Woe unto them that issue decrees of wickedness, and unto the scribes that always write anguish'; Jer. 8.8: 'How canst thou say, We are wise, and the law of JHWH is with us? Verily, the lying pen of the scribes has brought forth lies.'

[2] 'Das Buch der Könige . . . ', in *Eucharisterion*, 1923, p. 181

[3] Eissfeldt, *Einleitung*, 1934, p, 322; M. Noth, *Überlieferungsgeschichtliche Studien*, i, 1942, p. 73

kings mentioned in the annals also supports this supposition. The collection of the northern annals must thus have been saved from destruction after the death of Pekah, but before the fall of Samaria, by being transferred into the kingdom of Judah, which at this time had inherited a large number of northern traditions, e.g., the legends of Elijah and Elisha, the prophecies of Hosea, etc.

In Deuteronomy itself we find writing used for other purposes, in the administration of justice. Deut. 24.1 ff contains the decrees regarding divorce; here it is laid down that the man who wishes to be divorced must have a bill of divorcement drawn up—a practice that naturally dates from pre-exilic times, judging from the metaphorical use of the bill of divorcement in the prophets (Jer. 3.8; cf. also Isa. 50.1).

In Josh. 18.4 ff we read that Joshua sent men out to survey the remaining parts of the West Jordan country. He instructs them to note down the results of their survey so that these can be used in the division of the land between the tribes that as yet had received no territory. The text may be attributed to the most recent strata in the book of Joshua.[1]

The political central administration could not dispense with writing. From the time of David one or more 'sōpherīm' make their appearance at the royal courts, but these are evidently high officials and not merely clerks; otherwise we should hardly have been told their names. In any case it is well worth while to try to get a clear understanding of the functions of these men. Jer. 52.25 mentions a 'sōphēr śar haṣṣābhā'', or, judging by the phrase, a man who might be secretary to the general, but the parallel passage in II Kings 25.19 has 'hassō-phēr śar haṣṣābhā'', which furnishes this man with direct military authority. In both recensions of the text it is said of him, that it was he who 'caused the people of the land to be mustered', i.e. levied them for military service.[2] In the letters from the royal archives at Mari[3] a military person is mentioned

---

[1] Cf. Noth's commentary on the passage   [2] Cf. Ges.-Buhl s.v. ṣābhā', Hiph.
[3] The present Tell Ḥarīri on the middle course of the Euphrates. The archives which date from the eighteenth to seventeenth centuries and contain correspondence with Hammurabi of Babylon, are being published by G. Dossin, C.-F. Jean and J. R. Kupper.

by the title DUB.SAR = Acc. ṭupšarru, i.e. tablet-writer. In
T.C.L., xxiii, No. 13, 29 he is mentioned between the 'magnate
of the West' (GAL.MAR.TU) and 'captain and picked soldier';
his name was Mašum[1] and his special duty was to attend to the
'tēbībtum', a species of muster. This was held for each district[2]
and served several purposes; first of all the one of ascertaining
the number of men fit for service in the district concerned, and
thus determining the contingent the district could provide.
The conscripted soldiers had their names put down on lists
and were obliged to remain in their home districts.[3] If the
'scribe' Mašum is identical with the sender of letter No. 131
from *T.C.L.* xxiii, he also had regular military functions, for in
this letter he describes his relief of a town which was threatened
by 2000 Ḥabīru.[4] In this connection it is interesting to note
that a 'sōphēr' appears in one of the oldest texts in the Old
Testament, the Song of Deborah, Judges 5.14, and that he
evidently has a purely military function. But this can hardly
surprise us when we consider that the Amorite culture, as it is
revealed in the Mari texts, in many ways points forward to the
culture of the invading Israelites.[5] Nevertheless it is significant
that 'has-sōphēr' as a regular institution first makes its appearance in the time of David, II Sam. 8.17; in the sanctuary legend
of Jerusalem, II Sam. 24, we have a description of a census of
the people remarkable as something quite new, a quite un-
Israelite action; but it should be pointed out that David does
not execute it by means of a 'sōphēr', but with the aid of Joab

---

[1] *T.C.L.*, xxii, No. 60, 6   [2] *T.C.L.*, xxii, No. 62, 5 f
[3] Cf. W. von Soden, 'Die altbabylonische Briefarchiv von Mari', *Die Welt des
Orients*, 1947, pp. 187-204. I am grateful to Mr Læssøe of Copenhagen University for the above references to *T.C.L.* On 'tēbībtum' cf. C.-F. Jean in *R.A.*,
1948, pp. 140 ff and especially pp. 196 f, and J. R. Kupper in *Studia Mariana*,
1950, pp. 99-110.
[4] The letter has recently been translated by Albright in Pritchard, *A.N.E.T.*,
1950, p. 483. It is particularly interesting on account of its mention of signalling
by means of light, a species of telegraphy which is recorded in the O.T., Jer. 6.1,
as well as in Lachish letter No. 4, and in the Jewish tradition; cf. Rosh ha-Shanah,
2. 2 f. See H. Torczyner, *The Lachish Letters*, 1938, p. 83.
[5] Cf. 'banū-jamina' and Benjamites; the concluding of a covenant by sacrifice,
in Mari by the killing of an ass; cf. the name of the leading clan in the covenant town of Shechem, benē-Hamōr; the mention of a military leader with the
title 'dawidum', with which the Meša inscription's 'dwdh' (l. 12) may be compared; and finally the mention of the bands of Ḥabīru operating in several places,
cf. the Hebrews of the Passover legend.

and his men. The census has a military purpose; it is to muster the genuine Israelite citizens, 'gibbōrē-ḥayil', those who are to appear at the king's summons and who are subject to taxation.

It is characteristic of every ancient Near Eastern kingdom that its correspondence with the neighbouring kingdoms was extensive, and even though the Old Testament sources relate nothing whatever of such a diplomatic correspondence *from* the Israelite kings, we may surmise by analogy that, for instance, Solomon's messengers to King Hiram of Tyre were provided with letters, but in true oriental style as an aid to, and a means of control over, the orally delivered message.

The writing of letters is, however, expressly mentioned in the case of messages of a more private nature, but the known instances are all of a distinctly macabre nature. This is true both of David's letter written to Joab, the contents of which it was impossible to let the messenger deliver orally (II Sam. 11.14), and of Jezebel's letters to the elders of Jezreel expressing a desire to have Naboth slandered (I Kings 21.8). Jehu's letter to the elders of Samaria (II Kings 10.1 f) also belongs to the sphere of the nefarious and could not at that time be proclaimed in public with its exhortation to the leading men of the city to make an end of the ruling dynasty. Here the *written* message evidently plays a considerable role and therefore the letters are expressly mentioned.

Before leaving the Deuteronomistic historical compilation we must examine some passages a little more closely. These are some phrases in connection with the Song of Moses (Deut. 31 f) and Josh. 24.25 f (Joshua gives the people statutes and ordinances and writes 'these words in the book of the law of God'), and I Sam. 10.25 (Samuel publicly recites the 'mishpaṭ' of the kingdom before the people and enters it in a book which he lays before the face of YHWH, i.e. in a YHWH sanctuary); further, the well-known passages that expressly cite a written source for the lines quoted. These passages are Num. 21.14 citing 'the Book of the Wars of YHWH'; Josh. 10.13 and II Sam, 1.18, citing 'the Book of the Upright', as well as I Kings 8.13, citing 'the Book of Songs' (only in LXX, III Kings 8.53).

which commentators often propose to change to 'the Book of the Upright'.[1]

The first group of passages is in literary critical circles typically enough referred to different sources: Josh. 24.26 to 'E', I Sam. 10.25 is considered a later addition, Deut. 31.9 ff is denoted 'Dt' with the exception of the portion of this chapter dealing with the song of Moses which is referred to a special source 'X'. By mentioning 'ḥōk ū-mishpāṭ', Josh. 24.25, the group of passages clearly reveals its connection in tradition with Ex. 15.25, where it is stated that Moses at one of the springs in the Kadesh oasis gave the people 'ḥōk ū-mishpāṭ', a passage which is normally referred to 'J'. We will here ignore the distinction between sources, and instead indicate the significance of the fact that these references do not appear at chance points in Old Testament tradition, but at crucial moments in the history of Israel, where one epoch succeeds another.

As the first point in the history of Israel's law the Sinai-Kadesh tradition is mentioned with its fundamental revelation. The next point is Moses' farewell to the people in the country east of Jordan; the conquest of the land and then the assembly in Shechem form the third milestone; and finally as the fourth link in the chain comes the decisive step which makes Israel a state and introduces the monarchy. It is characteristic of all these traditions that the law is promulgated publicly and orally, and that it is afterwards written down, and that this document is deposited in a sanctuary of YHWH. So the tradition of a law-book found in a temple of YHWH, II Kings 22 f, does not come upon the reader of the Deuteronomistic history without the necessary preparation.

More interesting to us in this connection is the fact that the law-tradition is of a double nature. When once the law has been ratified in an assembly of the people on the basis of an oral promulgation, it is written down and deposited in the holy place. But this does not mean that the oral recitation of the law ceases. In Deut. 31.9-11 the responsible leaders of the people are commanded to see to it that the law is orally promulgated in the assembly of all Israel when the people are

---

[1] Cf. Kittel, *Bibl. Heb.*, 3rd ed., ad loc.

gathered together every seventh year at the feast of tabernacles before the face of YHWH in the place where He lets His name dwell. This double method of tradition reminds one strikingly of the mode of tradition of the Homeric poems.

Let us dwell a moment on the fact that this text has become a point of departure for an interesting hypothesis as to the function of the 'minor' Judges as 'law reciters'. The latter designation is taken from a culture which is geographically, as well as historically, quite remote from the Israelite, viz., that of ancient Iceland, which has parallels with ancient Israelite culture in other fields too. The credit for first making such a comparison between these two cultures belongs to A. Klostermann.[1] He finds points of similarity between the old Icelandic law-book 'Grágás' and Deuteronomy: they must both be considered largely as a reduction to writing of the public recital of the law, and in reality they are both old law plus commentary. The literary form of the Icelandic law-book, which betrays its oral past by the mnemotechnic arrangement of material, is explained by the position of law in life. After Ulfliot had established an initial constitution and judicial system, the transmission of the laws was attended to by men chosen for this office; these 'lögsögumaðr' had the office of reciting large portions of the law at the annual assemblies (called 'things'). With the changing times modifications and additions are introduced, 'Nymaeli' are added, but the law remains itself in its essence.[2] As to Deuteronomy we have from the surrounding texts the rule cited above which clearly states that the law is to be read every seventh year at the feast of Tabernacles. Moses' own oral declaration of the law is expressly designated in Deut. 1.5 as an explanation of the words of the law; according to tradition he combines in his person the functions of both the law-giver and the law reciter. He also resembles the Icelandic law reciter in that the more intricate legal decisions are reserved for him, Deut. 1.17, Ex. 18.22. Joshua must likewise be considered a law reciter, and

[1] *Der Pentateuch*, N. F., 1907, esp. pp. 348-428. Buhl says of Klostermann as a scholar in *Det israelitiske folks historie*, 7th ed., 1936, p. 15: 'he went his own ways far from the usual main paths of modern research.'
[2] *Op. cit.*, p. 415

he and Samuel are both said to have added 'Nymaeli' to the Mosaic codex, Jos. 24.25 f and I Sam. 10.25. Between Joshua and Samuel we have the 'minor' Judges,[1] men who were neither priests nor heroes, but who are remembered because they 'judged Israel'. We must regard these men as being full of understanding and well versed in the true tradition, and it was their privilege to convene and to lead general assemblies of the people. Almost thirty years later this hypothesis has been endorsed by Alt,[2] and it is shared by Noth,[3] who in this connection denies that the monarchy had any influence on the framing of Israelite law, as we find it in the Old Testament—a view which a closer analysis, however, will prove to be illusory.

The other group of passages seems to bear unmistakable witness to the fact that writing was already used for real literary purposes in early pre-exilic times. We have at least two different literary works mentioned by name, 'the Book of the Wars of YHWH' and 'the Book of the Upright'.

From 'the Book of the Upright' comes a verse which refers to Joshua's war against the Southern Canaanite coalition under the leadership of Adoni-zedek, king of Jerusalem, Josh. 10.13, and David's lament for Saul and Jonathan, II Sam. 1.18; and possibly also Solomon's words at the dedication of the temple at Jerusalem, I Kings 8.13. Already the fact that these poems —between the origin of which there may be several centuries —here stand side by side in the same work, so that an author writing in the sixth century can refer to them, must demand our attention and caution. Which is more likely, that at the time of Joshua one began to compile a work called 'the Book of the Upright', and through the centuries continued to add new material to it, or that the poems from the time of Joshua and later generations lived on the lips of the bards, until at some unknown time and from motives as to which we can

---

[1] Judges 10.1-5 and 12.7-15. They were six in number, were of distinguished rank and well-to-do. Jephthah, a half-blood, probably only attained to the dignity because he had previously been the deliverer. Shamgar did not belong to the 'minor' judges.

[2] *Die Ursprünge des isr. Rechts*, 1934, p. 31

[3] *Die Gesetze im Pentateuch*, 1940, p. 48. Noth urges the connection between the religious league of the twelve tribes which came into existence after the conquest, the amphictyony, and the O.T. laws.

only conjecture, these poems—chosen in the course of tradition
and time—were collected into a book, and called 'the Book of
the Upright'? I have no doubt but that the latter is the more
probable. Perhaps our conception is substantiated in another
way, by the words connected with David's lament for Saul
and Jonathan. We read in II Sam. 1.17 f: 'And David made
the following lamentation over the bodies of Saul and his son
Jonathan, and he commanded them to teach the children of
Judah a bow (?).' 'Kesheth' (bow) seems very peculiar here;
it is omitted in LXX and this has given rise to doubts as to the
integrity of the text.[1] The Massoretic text, which is *lectio diffi-
cilior* and is further supported by the Peshitta, must be retained;
it might be possible to understand 'Kesheth' as the name of
the poem in which the picture of Jonathan's bow occupies
such a prominent place. The words 'lelammēdh benē-Yehūdhāh'
do not in any case belong to the usual late headings with which
the Old Testament Psalms are so well supplied. It is only to
be found in one case, Ps. 60; more recent study of the Psalms
has attempted to move this Psalm back some 800 years, from
the time of the Maccabees to the time of David. 'Lammēdh'
means 'to impress upon others by oral teaching'; the word is
especially characteristic of the framework of Deuteronomy.

Thus the texts mentioned here can hardly *prove* that writing
was in use for literary purposes in early pre-exilic times, and
it is hardly advisable to *surmise* a literary activity of this kind
until the approach of the time when the culture as a whole
tended to a written fixation of its traditions.

In reality Num. 21.13-14 points in the same direction: 'From
thence they removed and pitched camp on the other side of
Arnon, which is in the wilderness that comes out from the
territory of the Amorites. Rightly is it said in the book of the
wars of YHWH, "Waheb in Sufa and the gorges, Arnon and the
slope of the gorges, which goes down to the seat of Ar and
leans toward the territory of Moab".' The quotation is evidently cited because of the last three or four words which show
that Arnon is the boundary river of Moab. It is clear that there

[1] Cf. Kittel, *Bibl. Heb.*, 3rd ed., and Gesenius-Buhl, *Handwörterbuch* s.v.
Kesheth

is no inner connection between a quotation from 'the Book of the Wars of YHWH', a travel record which gives the route from the wilderness of Sinai to the East Jordan country, and the account of the battles between the Moabites and the Amorites. This fragment of a song of victory[1] must—since it is an Israelite one—refer to the boundary between *Israel* and Moab. YHWH has given the people possession of the land of the Amorites; this is the narrator's presupposition and that is why he gives the quotation here. But typically enough he has not yet related that YHWH had given the land of the Amorites to Israel; this is first mentioned in vv. 21 f. Seen from the narrator's viewpoint—and still more from that of the tradition-ists—these events belong to the distant past; the 'territory of the Amorites' has long ago become the East Jordan possessions of Israel, and therefore it is affirmed on the evidence of the Book of the Wars of YHWH that the boundary of Moab really is Arnon. This quotation which establishes a boundary pre-supposes two things. (1) Israel must have become settled, and (2) the Moabites must have been forced back beyond Arnon. This situation does not arise in the time of the Judges, as the Moabites still possessed land beyond the Jordan, Judges 3.12. It is only under David that the Moabites are subdued (II Sam. 8.2), and subsequently by Omri (II Kings 3.4 f, and Mesha inscription, ll. 4-8). During or after the reign of Ahab, Moab advances again, and it is an open question whether still another Israelite king, viz. Jeroboam II, about the middle of the eighth century (II Kings 14.25), succeeded in driving the Moabites back beyond the Arnon.[2] At least after his time the Moabites

---

[1] Or a song of derision? Cf. Eissfeldt, *Einleitung*, 1934, pp. 99 f.

[2] Amos 6.14 indicates the extent of the kingdom at the time of this king in this way: 'From the entering in of Hamath unto the stream of Arabah', and II Kings 14.25 reads: 'He [Jeroboam II] restored the territory of Israel from the entering of Hamath unto the sea of Arabah, according to the word of YHWH, the God of Israel, which he spoke by his servant, the prophet Jonah b. Amittai, who, was of Gath-ha-Hepher.' While scholars are agreed that 'yām hā-'arābhāh' is a designation of the Dead Sea, it has been difficult to reach an agreement as to the location of 'naḥal hā-'arābhāh' (cf. Hammershaimb, *Amos*, 1946, pp. 104 f). It is most reasonable to surmise that 'naḥal hā-'arābhāh' must be a stream or river flowing into the Dead Sea. When it is used as a designation of the southern boundary of Israel in such a lapidary passage, it must be a stream of some significance in the minds of the people, and it was perhaps considered the ideal boundary for Israel; cf. the parallel text in II Kings 14.25: 'He *restored* . . . ' I

rule the territories north of the Arnon, for Isa. 15 mentions Nebo, Medeba, Heshbon, and Jahaz as towns of Moab. Thus, the quotation in Num. 21.14 can originate from any of three epochs in the history of Israel, the time of David, Omri, or Jeroboam II. Now II Kings 14.25 states expressly that the victories of Jeroboam II to the north-east and the south-east were accomplished according to the word of a prophet of YHWH;[1] is it not natural then to see a connection between this quotation from 'the Book of the Wars of YHWH' and Jonah b. Amittai? Perhaps the objection will be raised that it is a strangely reversed method of procedure to try to 'confirm' older traditions by younger ones. Quite apart from the fact that such things may be pointed out in other cases too in the Old Testament,[2] one must remember the Israelite's attitude towards tradition. It is to him a world from which his life draws nourishment; he lives in it, is strengthened in it, and it gives him a goal for his exertions. Therefore it is only a half truth that in Num. 21 it is the old traditions that are supported by a new, it is just as true that it is the present situation of the Israelite which is supported by the traditions of the past, 'Rightly is it said in the book of the wars of YHWH . . . '

There remains the question of the character of this book from which the quotation is taken. If it is true that the quotation is rhythmical, that we here have a fragment of a song of victory or a song of derision, 'the Book of the Wars of YHWH' may to a certain degree be considered a parallel to 'the Book of the Upright'. The latter is a collection of songs, apparently

therefore suggest that 'naḥal hā-arābhāh' should be considered a poetic circumlocution for the Arnon, especially as Amos in his threats against Moab only mentions one Moabite town (Amos 2.2), probably the capital of Moab proper, Qeriyoth, presumably identical with the Ar of Isa. 15.1, and certainly situated south of the Arnon, but he does not mention either Mēdebā, 'Ataroth, or Dībōn, all situated north of the Arnon. According to his inscription, ll. 9 f, Mesha recaptured these towns from Israel. If these towns had belonged to Moab, when Amos was active in Bethel, he would surely have mentioned them in the passage above; the analogy with the other words of Amos in chapters 1-2 go to prove this. At any rate we venture to conclude that Jeroboam II really had succeeded in driving the Moabites out.

[1] Cf. preceding note

[2] Thus the episode Jer. 26.20-24 can hardly have taken place before the events mentioned in 26.1-19. But the episode is related in order to throw the risk Jeremiah ran into relief. Cf. also Acts. 5.34 f.

of Southern, Judaean origin, while 'the Book of the Wars of YHWH' according to the presentation above must be considered a collection of North Israelite poems. It can presumably at the earliest have been completed towards the end of Jeroboam II's reign, and at the latest before the fall of Samaria. This brings us to a time disturbed by the onslaught of Assyria in the West, and it is quite possible that a feeling of crisis spread in some circles of the Israelite people, and that the glorious traditions and oracles slowly began to be written down.[1]

There is no room here for a comprehensive account of the use the prophets made, or did not make, of writing in pre-exilic times. Later we will discuss the important text, Jer. 36, and give a sample of traditio-historical exegesis of a collection of oracles, Mic. 4-5. For the present we will restrict ourselves to referring those interested to the already mentioned dissertations by Birkeland, Mowinckel, and Engnell. But in connection with what we have said above about the importance of a feeling of political crisis as a motive for the increase of literary activity, we would like to raise the supplementary question: Why does 'written' prophecy begin with precisely Amos and Hosea in the northern kingdom and with Isaiah in the southern kingdom? The consummate literary form of their books shows clearly that they cannot be regarded merely as an incipient beginning of something completely new. And yet since the victory of the historico-critical method of Bible research in the last century the most common conception is that with Amos something quite new and exceptional comes into being in world history, personality-religion is fashioned by these men's experiences of God in a world and a community, the religion of which might be characterized as 'static nature religion'.[2] Due only to the circumstance that the prophets

---

[1] In *Z.A.W.*, N.F. xii, pp. 130-152: 'Hat es ein israelitisches Nationalepos gegeben?', Mowinckel assumes the identity of these two collections. His argument rests on an assumption which it is easier to refute than to prove: that Num. 21.17 also is a quotation from the 'Book of the Wars of YHWH'. In his article he emphasizes the oral tradition as well as the late composition of the work.

[2] That this conception has lasted until our own time is evident from a chapter which is strangely 'out of fashion' in many regards, 'Jeremia og Religionshistorien', the introductory chapter to H. Birkeland's book on Jeremiah, 1950 (in the series 'Religionens stormenn'). He overlooks almost entirely the connection

themselves saw to it that their works were published,[1] we have a large portion of their preaching preserved. An attempt has been made to prove their creative contribution in the *literary* field, but our increasing acquaintance with the literature of the ancient Near East as well as our revised conception of the date of the origin of, e.g. the Israelite psalms, together with our changing conception of the relation of the prophets to the cult,[2] is a definite argument to the contrary. The prophets were supposed to be revolutionary in their *ethical* preaching. This viewpoint is, however, only tenable so long as one regards the Israelite *laws* as late pre-exilic literature, reflecting the prophetic message in many points. But who in our days dare acknowledge the view that God as a God of righteousness is a theological tenet created by the later Israelite prophets? The prologue to Codex Hammurabi (1.32 f) says that the gods have made Hammurabi king 'in order to let righteousness shine forth in the land, to abolish the wicked and the criminal, so that the mighty shall not abuse the weak', and in the epilogue we read (XXIV.59-62): 'in order that the mighty shall not oppress the weak, and that orphans and widows may receive justice.' Hence the new contribution of prophetism was thought to consist in the fact that these men were so imbued with righteousness on behalf of YHWH that they had to preach the *uncompromising judgement* of the apostate people. Their entirely unique message was thought to be this: YHWH had finally rejected His people because of their sins. But this interpretation can only be maintained by first casting suspicion on the 'positive statements' in Amos (9.11-15), Hos. (2), Isa. (2.1-4, 9, 11, etc.) and Mic. (2.12-13, 4-5), or re-interpreting them (Isa. 7). Instead one ought to try to find something that is common to at least the main portion of the collections of prophetic oracles which have been handed down to us, something that

of the later Israelite prophets with earlier Israelite prophetism and prophetism in the surrounding countries, and thus obscures the structure of later Israelite prophetism.

[1] Birkeland, *op. cit.*, modifies this and says there were at least some who understood, or thought they understood, these new men, and therefore passed on their words until they were finally written down: see p. 9

[2] It should be superfluous to point out that a new departure in this field was made by S. Mowinckel in his *Psalmenstudien*, I-VI, 1921-24

in a characteristic way distinguishes the preaching of these men from that of such men as Ahijah of Shiloh (I Kings 14), Micaiah b. Imlah (I Kings 22), Elijah (I Kings 17 ff) and Elisha (I Kings 19 ff) as well as from the prophets in the countries surrounding Israel. This is the line that has been attempted by scholars in modern times. I may here refer to Engnell's paper on 'Profetismens ursprung och uppkomst',[1] where he points out that the common ground for prophets such as Amos and Hosea is their preaching of Jerusalem's YHWH and their struggle for the Jerusalem kingship. Their preaching may be called genuinely Israelite in so far as they stand in the main current of Israel's own religious history, that of Jerusalem and Deuteronomy. As a genuinely Israelite prophet in this sense Amos is 'perhaps . . . not the first but the first we have any certain knowledge of'.[2] And now we proceed to the answer to our question. If this Jerusalem-Deuteronomic tendency can be discovered also in the written prophets from the time before the exile, it is comprehensible why the words of just these prophets have survived; especially considering the fact that the centuries in which they were active are remarkable for the fall of the northern kingdom, its destruction as an independent state and, as a consequence of this, the rising hopes of the Judaeans for the re-establishment of the kingdom of David under the leadership of Jerusalem[3] (Amos 9.11 ff, Mic. 5.2 ff, Isa. 7, Jer. 3, etc.). This does not imply that the preaching of Jeremiah, for instance, is exhaustively characterized. He preaches judgement and righteousness as well, and as poet and lyricist he represents the acme in Old Testament literature. But the fact that his prophecies have been preserved is presumably due not so much to these factors as to the fact that the 'Deuteronomists' were able to use his message because his hopes of a reunion of the two brother-nations merely represents the leading thought of the Deuteronomist, expressed in another way.

We conclude this section on the use of writing in pre-exilic

[1] In *Religion och Bibel*, 1949, pp. 1-18
[2] *Op. cit.*, p. 18
[3] As long as the northern kingdom existed as an independent state these hopes were in vain; cf. 2 Kings 14.8 f (Amaziah of Judah and Joash of Israel)

Israel by inquiring whether archaeology has anything to say in confirmation or refutation of our thesis.

So far no inscriptions, tablets or documents from pre-exilic times have been found in Palestine which might be designated as Israelite literature. The epigraphical material we have is easily surveyed: ostraca from Samaria, informing us of the Israelite court household of the time of Jeroboam II, and from the time of Hezekiah the Siloam inscription which relates an episode from the completion of this undertaking. Above all we have from the last days of the kingdom of Judah the Lachish letters, ostraca sent to the Judaean commander Ya'ōsh in Lachish, the present Tell ed-Duweir.[1] These letters are indeed not without importance for our subject as they seem to give us some notion of the ability to read and write in this period. Letter No. 3, lines 8-13, reads:

(8) וכי אמר · אדני · לא · ידעתה ·

(9) קרא ספר חיהוה · אם · נסה · א

(10) יש לקרא לי ספר לנצח · וגם ·

(11) כל ספר אשר יבא · אלי אם ·

(12) קראתי · אתה · · ראת מנהו

(13) כל · מאום[2]

The letter has been variously interpreted, and this is true of the letter as a whole as well as of the lines quoted here. We cite one of the earliest and one of the most recent translations, by Torczyner and Albright.

On Torczyner's rendering,[3] Ya'ōsh, the commandant of Lachish, has sent a letter to the sender of this letter, Hōsha'yāhū and dwelt on the fact: 'that he says: My Lord, I do not know to read a letter. Yahweh lives (to punish me) if anybody has tried to read to me a letter for ever. And also, whatever letter came to me I have not read it and not even seen anything of it.' On this Torczyner makes the following remark: 'It is certainly not a matter of course that everybody could read and write at that time.' To a passage in letter No. 4, which was presumably

---

[1] The letters are edited by H. Torczyner, *The Lachish Letters*, 1938. The relevant literature is becoming quite voluminous.

[2] Torczyner, *op. cit.*, Plates on pp. 46-47

[3] Torczyner, p. 51, Commentary p. 65

sent by the same Hōsha'yāhū and reads: 'I have written on the page according to whatever my lord has sent to me', Torczyner remarks: ' "I have written" must certainly not be meant as "written by my hand", but may well be "made (my scribe) write" as in many similar examples in the Bible and in all ancient literature' (see Jer. 30.2, 36.19, 51.59-62).[1]

The rendering of ידעתה by the first person singular has, however, been disputed and is hardly correct. Albright's translation reads thus: 'And as for what my Lord said, "Dost thou not understand?—call a scribe!" As Yahweh liveth no one hath ever undertaken to call a scribe for me; and as for any scribe who might have come to me, truly I did not call him nor would I give anything at all for him!'[2] Here לא ידעתה is construed as a question, ספר is vocalized 'sōphēr' instead of 'sēpher'. Both these interpretations show clearly and unmistakably that writing belonged to the craftsman, even when it was a case of the relatively simple Canaanite alphabetic writing (in which the Lachish letters are written), and that even men of authority[3] were—or could be conceived of as—illiterate. Could one wish for any better confirmation of Nyberg's words: 'The art of writing was the business of the "ḥāṣṣat" (the specialist) and not that of the "'ammat" (the layman), as it always has been in the east.'[4]

2. We may now briefly consider the other side of our problem, and seek the positive evidence for the existence of an oral tradition in Israel. In the case of the legal material we have already touched on the importance of oral tradition in connection with Klostermann's hypothesis regarding Deuteronomy and the minor Judges. To be sure we regard it as impossible to consider the Deuteronomy we know as a sample of pre-exilic literature—for instance, as being identical with Josiah's law-book from 622 B.C. It should, however, be possible to speak of a Deuteronomistic trend in the culture of pre-exilic Israel, and its first origin should be sought—in agreement with Noth—in the sacred institution which consti-

---

[1] No. 4, Plates on pp. 76-77, ll. 3-4, Commentary p. 81
[2] In Pritchard's *A.N.E.T.*, 1950, p. 322
[3] Hōsha'yāhū presumably held military rank
[4] *Studien zum Hoseabuche*, p. 8

tuted itself under the name of Israel as a union of twelve tribes, an amphictyony, in central Palestine (cf. Josh. 24). The Deuteronomic laws may in the course of time have developed from the oral recitation of laws, periodically held in the Israelite assemblies. If we consider Deuteronomy itself it is immediately and forcibly impressed upon us that the introductory as well as the concluding parenetical sections were based on the oral recitation of the laws.

(*a*) Deut. 1.5 itself indicates the entire following work as Moses' own oral, expository recitation of the law. Deut. 4.1 depicts the situation: 'Now therefore hearken, O Israel, unto the statutes and judgements, which I teach you, to do them, that ye may live, and go in and possess the land which YHWH, the God of your fathers gives you.' Or 4.8: 'And what nation is there so great, that hath statutes and judgements so righteous as all this law, which I set before you *this day*?' Furthermore, 4.20: 'But the Lord hath taken you and brought you forth out of the iron furnace, even out of Egypt, to be unto him a people of his own inheritance, as ye are *this day*.' Or again, 4.38-40*a*: (YHWH led the people forth out of Egypt) 'to drive out nations from before thee greater and mightier than thou art, to bring thee in, to give thee their land for an inheritance as it is *this day*. Know therefore *this day* and consider it in thy heart, that YHWH is God in heaven above and upon earth beneath; there is none else. Thou shalt keep therefore his statutes and his commandments which I command thee *this day* . . . ' The entire fourth chapter with its ever recurrent 'this day' reflects its use at the assemblies.

(*b*) But we can define a little more precisely the cultic aspect of this 'assembly' which in Deut. 31.11 is expressly stated to take place at the feast of Tabernacles, or in other words at the New Year festival, the autumn festival, which after the introduction of the monarchy was the royal festival proper in Israel. In the slightly historicized introduction to the Decalogue we still clearly perceive the cultic actualization of the creative deeds of the past: 'And Moses called all Israel and said unto them: "Hear, O Israel, the statutes and judgements which I speak in your ears this day, and ye shall learn them and keep them so

that ye do them. YHWH our God made a covenant with us in
Horeb. Not with our fathers made YHWH this covenant, but
with us, even us who are all of us alive this day" ' (Deut. 5.1-3).
If Psalm 95 is an enthronement psalm, the passage 'To-day
when ye hear his voice, harden not your hearts as in Meri-
bah . . . ' (vv. 7-8) throws an interesting light on this festival
of the covenant and popular assembly.[1] A festival of the
covenant coinciding with a royal festival must certainly be
interpreted in this way: the king is recognized as being responsible for God's law to the people. Seen against our knowledge of the religious conditions of the kings of Israel and
Judah, influenced as it is by the Deuteronomist, this may seem
strange to us. Yet it is no more remarkable than that Hammurabi holds the same position as an intermediate between Marduk
—or Shamash if one prefers—and his subjects.[2]

(c) But the Old Testament also assumes a transmission of
the law which is not connected with the great festivals or
sanctuaries alone, the father's oral teaching of his household,
and especially of his sons. There is direct evidence of this in
our texts, and there is not the slightest reason to deny that such
a teaching in the home took place in a community permeated
to the core by patriarchal ideas. The home is a miniature
national community. Just as the people may be said to be
concentrated in a single individual, the chieftain or the king,
who in himself bears the destiny of the people and whose acts
have consequences for the future of the whole people, so too
the *pater familias* is 'the centre from which strength and will
emanate through the whole of the sphere which belongs to
him and to which he belongs'.[3] Just as the community on
certain occasions is confronted by the fundamental principles
of its existence, so too is the family (cf. Ex. 12.26; 13.8, 14;
Deut. 4.9-10; 6.7, 20 f, etc.).

[1] On the connection of Psalm 95 with the festival of the covenant and the
transmission of the law, see for instance Mowinckel, *Le Décalo ue*, 1927, pp.
121-133
[2] On the king as the bearer of the law, see, e.g. Östborn, *Tōrā in the Old
Testament*, 1945, ch. 3. Cf. too my article: 'The Righteous and the Wicked in
the Book of Habaqquq', *Studia Theologica*, VI, i, 1953, pp. 54 ff.
[3] Johs. Pedersen, *Israel: its Life and Culture*, I-II, 1926, p. 63

In this connection it would be natural to glance at the Wisdom literature, which by the teacher's fatherly relation to his pupil reveals a spiritual affinity to the father's teaching of his sons. It becomes more and more apparent that this type of literature extended through the whole ancient Orient and was exceedingly old; it was especially cultivated in the schools as a special type, and was thus presumably from the very first intimately connected with the art of writing and the scribes.[1] If we examine the book of Proverbs with this in mind we shall undoubtedly be surprised to note that in one place only in all these collections is the use of writing directly affirmed, Prov. 22.20: 'Do I not write to thee "thirty", with counsel and knowledge?', and that this passage in all probability refers to the Egyptian book of Wisdom, which bears the name of Amen-em-ope. For this book contains exactly thirty chapters, and a portion of their contents is given in the immediately following section of Proverbs. On the other hand we find the expression 'to write upon the tablets of one's heart' in several places (3.1 f and 7.1 f). This phrase must be compared with the Arabic expression about the Qurân, that it 'lives in the hearts of the believers', i.e. they know it by heart.[2] Besides this, Proverbs contains direct evidence of the oral form of teaching, as when we read in 1.5:

'The wise man shall hear and increase his knowledge,
the man of understanding shall attain unto the art of living'

and also in 2.1 f:

'My son, when thou receivest my words
and hidest my commandments with thee
by opening thine ear to wisdom,
and applying thy thought to understanding . . . '[3]

Finally we may briefly mention that the book of Proverbs ends with a poem, the stanzas of which are arranged alphabetically, i.e. according to the initial letter of the stanza. This

[1] There is a detailed monograph on this subject by L. Dürr, *Das Erziehungswesen im Alten Testament und im Antiken Orient*, M.V.Å.G., xxxvi, 2, 1932
[2] Johs. Pedersen, *Den arabiske Bog*, 1946, p. 14
[3] Cf. further 4.1-5, 5.1-2, 6.21 and 8.1 f

is interesting evidence of the fact that the circles that were familiar with the art of writing did not reject the oral method of transmission. For it is difficult to imagine any other reason for an alphabetical composition and arrangement of the stanzas in this manner than the wish to procure a mnemonic aid.

The views that are here applied to the Proverbs are undoubtedly also valid to a certain extent for the Israelite book of Psalms. Since we are so fortunate as to possess parallel psalms in the book of Psalms and these are not quite identical in their present textual form, we can by examining these variants establish errors of hearing and thus prove that the oral tradition played its part in the composition of the Israelite Psalms.[1]

As to the prophetic and historical literature I shall attempt in the next chapter to make some analyses which should demonstrate what is characteristic of the traditio-historical method. Among recent traditio-historical discussions of the Old Testament historical books we may especially mention A. S. Kapelrud, *The Question of Authorship in the Ezra Narrative*, 1944.

3. We have attempted to establish the insignificant role of writing in pre-exilic Israel, and we have drawn forth some more or less unmistakable testimonies to the importance of oral transmission, testimonies taken from the Old Testament itself. And at the same time we have indicated reasons for the fact that writing at a certain epoch in the history of Israelite-Judaean culture gains an importance as a preserver of tradition which it had not earlier had in even approximately the same degree. To conclude we will briefly sum up these indications.

The change from oral to written literature does not take place because cultural summits have been reached, nor because the ability to read and write has become common property, but because the culture itself is felt to be threatened—from within by syncretism, and from without by political events.

[1] An analysis of this nature is H. Ringgren, 'Oral and Written Tradition' *Studia Theologica*, III, i, 1951, pp. 34-59

This change occurred, for Judah, presumably towards the end of the seventh century or at the beginning of the sixth, for northern Israel, perhaps a century and a half earlier. But it is neither consummated all at once nor does it put an end to oral transmission. To be sure there is a characteristic difference between the way in which Jeremiah is entrusted with the words of YHWH, and the way in which Ezekiel is charged with them (Jer. 1.9; Ezek. 2.8-3.9); and certainly it is symptomatic that it is precisely in Ecclesiastes that we find a phrase such as: 'And further, my son, be admonished! there is no end of the many books that are written, and much study wearies the flesh', and that the book of Esther alone contains one and a half times as many allusions to the use of writing as the whole Tetrateuch, though the latter fills twenty times as much space in the Hebrew Bible. Nevertheless, scarcely any other period can equal the oral tradition of Judaism as it has been deposited in the Talmud.[1]

It would lead too far here to demonstrate what forces and motives cause the formation of a written canon and a 'supplementary' oral tradition in one and the same period. One has the feeling that when once society has been somewhat consolidated through the incipient formation of a written canon, there is again room for oral tradition, and in this case its task will be to adjust an authoritative basis for the life of the community—which is now fixed in writing—to living conditions that have changed in the meantime. In this way history has evidently repeated itself many times; the Church and Islam are both outstanding examples of this. When one comes to think of it, it is a strange phenomenon that a writing or a collection of writings at some period in the history of a movement, a community, a confession, or a church, is canonized and that in future it maintains the character of a binding authority. Judaism, which has formed a school in this field, may perhaps have remembered forerunners of the canon from the earlier history of Israel. But whether the absolute validity which is attached to writing in theology—and which is practically manifested by the care of the Massoretes for the text—

[1] For literature, cf. above p. 21, n. 2

can be explained by Israel's own history, is perhaps rather doubtful.[1]

[1] It is a well-known fact that Mohammedan theologians consider the Qurân an earthly copy of the heavenly book. Related conceptions may be found in the Old Testament, most clearly in Ezekiel's vision at his call where the prophet describes how a book is given to him to eat and in it sighs and woe were written. This is of course the prophecy of doom for which he was to be a mouthpiece in the ensuing days. The Old Testament also speaks of heavenly books in quite a different way: of God's own book of doom in which the iniquities of every man are entered (Isa. 65.6 f), and of the heavenly census-paper in which the true worshippers of YHWH are written, and where their names can be blotted out if they turn aside from Him (cf. Ezek. 13.1 f; Ex. 32.32 f; Isa. 4.3; Mal. 3.16; Ps. 40.7, 69.28). In 'Mesopotamian Theology III', *Orientalia*, xix, No. 2, 1950, pp. 155 ff, A. Leo Oppenheim refers to the conclusion of the Irra myth as a proof that Mesopotamian theologians were not unacquainted with the conception of a heavenly book. The God Išum showed the poet in a vision the poem about Irra, and in the morning the poet wrote it down without adding or omitting a single word. The already mentioned colophon from a hymn to Ea, Shamash, Marduk, and Sin contains the technical word for a canonical, authoritative text, GAB.RI la-bi-ru. Cf. *A.f.O.*, xii, p. 245. This reference I owe to Mr. J. Læssøe.

IV

EXAMPLES OF TRADITIO-HISTORICAL
METHOD

In this concluding chapter on oral tradition we will turn directly to the Old Testament texts. Through their exegesis we shall attempt to show that the traditio-historical view of Old Testament literature involves a treatment of the texts which differs in a characteristic way from the literary-critical method.

To avoid misconceptions let us at once stress the fact that the traditio-historical method is *fundamentally* neither more nor less critical or conservative towards tradition than literary criticism is. The Old Testament scholar as a traditio-critic will be engrossed in the same task as the literary critic was and is, namely, a correct and true placing of the separate Old Testament texts. But *practically*, the traditio-historian is undoubtedly more reverent towards tradition. Not that he is more religious or more pious than the literary critic. His reverence and respect for tradition is merely an expression of the fact that he believes the creators of our written Old Testament capable of better things than mere editorial clumsiness; capable of more than merely lacking congeniality with the men from whom the material originally derives. In reality the traditio-historian gives these men credit for so much human dignity that he attempts with all his might to reach an understanding of the (sensible) motives that asserted themselves in the formation of large complexes of traditions.[1] However strange it may sound he can accept some of the detailed work of the literary critic. But to demand that he should merely continue to build on the old foundation laid by the literary critics, would be just as absurd as to demand that, for instance, an archaeologist should be able to use Doré's illustrated Bible as a handbook in biblical

---

[1] As, for instance, Ex. 1-15, 19-24, 32-34; Gen. 6-9; Isa. 6-9; Gen. 1-3; Mic. 1-3, 4-5; etc.

archaeology by merely retouching it here and there.[1] He
cannot merely continue the work of the literary critic. However
much their intentions may be the same, their methods remain
too different—first of all because the traditio-historian has
consciously come to a conclusion regarding the cultural presuppositions that belong to his own time, as well as that of the
literary critic. All this we have tried to emphasize in the
preceding chapters. We will now try to demonstrate this
difference in method by examples from a prophetic complex of
traditions and a complex of traditions from Genesis. For these
examples we have chosen some texts where the literary critical
treatment appears in a very characteristic way, and texts whose
problems the literary critics themselves believed they had
solved in a conclusive manner. But first we will turn to a
prophetic text that for generations has been considered a first
class source of information as to the origin of a prophetic book,
Jer. 36.

Jeremiah 36

It is the year 605 B.C. Assyria, the tyrant of Israel for a
century and a half, had been decisively defeated, and the
victor, Nebuchadrezzar, had beaten Assyria's ally, Pharaoh
Necho, in the battle of Carchemish in northern Syria. A great
power to the north and one to the south, and Syria and Palestine as a common sphere of interest and battleground—an old
familiar story!

The international conflict had already in 609 dealt Judah a
heavy blow with the fall of Josiah at Megiddo. We know that
his kingdom was of a considerable size, for according to the
account of his reform, II Kings 22 f, Josiah had been able to
extend his power unhindered to the old northern Israelite
sanctuary, Bethel. But his defeat meant—at any rate at first—
a position of dependence upon Egypt. So the kingdom of
Judah would from the outset be an interested spectator of the
trial of strength at Carchemish.

In this very year, the fourth year of the reign of King
Jehoiakim, the YHWH prophet Jeremiah comes forward with

---

[1] The illustration has been chosen at random and must not be pressed

oracles of misfortune against Judah's own king. His whole message from his call in the days of King Josiah to the present is written down and read first to the people, then to the officials, and finally to the king himself, three times on the same day. The king's only reaction to these prophecies is the wish to get rid of the prophecy—and the prophet. He deliberately causes the roll to be burned, piece by piece, and gives orders to arrest Jeremiah and his disciple Baruch. But YHWH protects his prophet, and hides him from his pursuers and commands him to make another roll; this Jeremiah does, 'and there were added besides unto them many like words'.

The chapter is clearly divided into three sections: 1-8, 9-26, 27-32. All three sections have in common that each is a complete entity in itself, but at the same time they are mutually interdependent like three links in a chain. The account is characterized by excellent Israelite narrative art.

There is no serious reason for doubting the correctness of the introductory indication of time; the all-important event of this year renders Jeremiah's youthful prophecy of 'disaster from the north' topical. In this year 605 the word of YHWH came to Jeremiah telling him to write down 'all the oracles that I have spoken unto thee against Israel, and against Judah, and against all the nations' from the call of the prophet in the days of Josiah 'until this day'. And furthermore the reason why he should take all this upon himself, unprecedented though it apparently is, is given: Judah is to repent because of his words so that YHWH can forgive them. Jeremiah is to appear before the people as a last warning, a last attempt to restore the broken covenant.

We ask why it is absolutely necessary for Jeremiah to *write down* his oracles. Why is it not sufficient for him to deliver them orally? If he has been able to retain his prophecies for more than twenty years without the aid of writing, why must he resort to it now? It is possible that the first listeners to the narrator to whom we owe this account asked this question too, just as they marvelled at the command given to Jeremiah to place a loin-cloth in a gorge by the Euphrates (ch. 13). But there, as here, the course of events gives the answer—

E

the oracle only awakes wonder and the desire to hear more.

Obedient to the oracle Jeremiah has the scribe (36.4) Baruch-ben-Neriah-ben-Mahseiah (32.12) write down from his own dictation all the words he, Jeremiah, has received from YHWH. Unfortunately we do not know whether this is Jeremiah's first meeting with Baruch—if so it made them friends until the death of Jeremiah—or whether Baruch was already closely associated with Jeremiah; ch. 45 leaves both possibilities open. However, in all probability Baruch belonged to the circle that we by force of analogy must surmise existed around the great prophet.[1]

We read further (v. 5) that Jeremiah is prevented from going to the Temple and therefore commands Baruch to go instead. We begin to understand why Jeremiah had to have the prophecies written down. If Baruch is 'new to the service' there is—it would seem—a natural reason for having it written down. Although the oral form of teaching was prevalent and preferred in the ancient Orient, a new disciple might well need the aid of a written text to help him in his recitation—at least that is the way we reason on the basis of our cultural suppositions. But if Baruch already belonged to Jeremiah's band of disciples, and was perhaps even his favourite disciple[2] or something similar, this would in reality appear to be superfluous. In this case it would be reasonable to assume that the disciple was just as familiar with the tradition as his master; the function of the disciples was precisely to preserve the tradition.[3]

It might be conjectured that the command to write down the prophecy was motivated by the desire to preserve the prophecy for later generations (cf. Isa. 30.8 and Jer. 32.14).

[1] Van der Ploeg ('Le rôle de la tradition orale', *R.B.*, liv, 1947, p. 36) emphasizes the fact that Baruch is the only disciple mentioned. 'The book of Jeremiah does not mention (other disciples), but on the contrary, it describes the prophet as a lonely man . . . ' But is not this one of those *argumenta e silentio* which are 'toujours faible' (cf. p. 37)? For one cannot base a conception of Jeremiah as the 'great lonely man' on a rhetorical phrase such as 15.17*b*, the content and significance of which is fully explained by the previous half verse.

[2] Engnell, 'Profetia och Tradition', *S.E.Å.*, 1947, p. 129

[3] Mowinckel (*N.T.T.*, 1942, pp. 78 f) also sees the reason for writing down the prophecy in the fact that Jeremiah was prevented. The more detailed motivation, that the roll was to serve as an aid to memory and insure a 'recitation as fluent and effective as possible', seems a little too modern, although it cannot be excluded in advance.

But this is quite foreign to the point of view of our narrator. The aim of the whole action is to make an impression on the present generation, and make them return to YHWH so that He will repent of His wrath before it is too late.

Baruch acts as Jeremiah's messenger and his ambassador in cases where Jeremiah cannot appear himself. And here the motive for v. 2 must be found. The messenger must have a credential, a document, so that the correctness of his message may be controlled, and it may be known that he speaks in another's name. The same principle applies here as in the case of correspondence between the courts of the ancient Orient.

Why Jeremiah was prevented from going to the Temple himself we do not know, but that is of subordinate importance to the narrative. Baruch is to go to the Temple on a day of fast because his audience would be largest on such an occasion and probably be most receptive to Jeremiah's words of doom. The first section of the narrative closes with the remark about Baruch's complete obedience to Jeremiah's command; it is in fact rounded off by v. 8. Anticipation as to the future course of events is great, and the detailed account now follows in the main section. Using a term well known from Gunkel's commentary on Genesis we might call vv. 1-8 the exposition, the starting point for the actual course of events.

An occasion presents itself in the ninth month of the following year. Presumably the New Year is here reckoned from the spring festival, so that this is in the month of December (cf. v. 22). If the early rains had failed famine was to be feared and this may have caused the proclamation of a day of fast.[1] Jeremiah had influential friends among the old officials from the days of the pious King Josiah, and these put a doorway to a cell at the disposal of Baruch,[2] so that he could fulfil his mission easily and have as large an audience as possible. And now events follow without intermission. First, the common people hear the roll, but we hear nothing of its effect. In spite of v. 3 and v. 7 this is outside the aim of the recital. We are only told that the recital makes an impression on one person,

[1] Cf. for instance Rudolph's commentary, ad loc.
[2] This must be the meaning of the text

Micaiah, a son of one of the old officials. When we read the following verses we receive the impression that these old officials stick together and cleave to the traditions from the time of Josiah: they sit together in the chamber of the scribe[1] and they at once send for Baruch, prompted by Micaiah's account. If Micaiah's account makes a deep impression upon them, then Baruch's recitation makes a still deeper; they look at each other in terror, and together with Baruch they consider whether they should give Jeremiah's message to the king.[2] And when they have established the authenticity of the roll they go to Jehoiakim and inform him of the day's event. But the attention of the listeners is further excited, for in v. 19 it says: 'And the officials said unto Baruch: Go, hide thee, thou and Jeremiah, and let no man know where ye are,' and in v. 20: 'but they left the roll in the chamber of Elishama the scribe.' Even though one knew nothing of King Jehoiakim before, and though one had no concrete ideas of the contents of the roll, we now suspect that the possibility of a conflict is present. And with this suspicion we listen to the climax of the drama.

The next scene is very concentrated. Here the opposition between two parties is depicted in a way which is reminiscent of the technique of the Deuteronomist's historical compilation (cf. I Kings 12 and 18): on the one hand the prophet zealous for YHWH, and his adherents with their sincere respect for his prophecy and their solicitude for his person, and on the other the young king and his youthful counsellors. The king is not satisfied with a second-hand account of the affair, but commands that the roll itself be brought. In a few short sentences the situation is depicted for the listeners, all that is necessary for vv. 23 f is said here, and then we are told: 'And when Jehudi had read three or four columns he (Jehoiakim) cut it off with the penknife and cast it into the fire in the brazier. Yet they were not afraid, nor rent their garments, neither the king nor any of his ministers that heard all these words; and though

---

[1] That this was a cabinet meeting as often stated in commentaries is rather improbable, considering that the king's closest counsellors are absent. Cf. above as to the scribe.

[2] Thus M.T. There is no reason for preferring the Septuagint's rendering which avoids the rare, but not unique, construction 'pāḥadhū 'īsh 'el-rēʿēhū'.

Elnathan, and Delaiah, and Gemariah earnestly interceded with the king that he would not burn the roll, yet he would not hear them' (23-25).

In v. 16 we were told that these 'Josian' officials looked at each other in terror, and already at this point we think of the account in II Kings 22 of the effect of the law-book on Josiah and his men. But here the allusion is still more plain. It is an antithesis not only to v. 16, but to II Kings 22.11: 'And when the king [Josiah] had heard the words of the law-book, he rent his clothes.' Accordingly we need not be in doubt as to which circles composed the narrative. Indeed, this, the culmination of ch. 36 is marked by the very best in Hebrew narrative technique; brief, concise, and concentrated without wallowing in sentiment of any kind. Thus the narrator tells his story, only indirectly revealing the horror of the old men and the deliberate audacity of the young men. And once again, as in the beginning of the story, the listeners cannot avoid asking themselves why Jehoiakim acts in such a way. It was something that was expected when we heard of the precautionary measures of the old men, but there has been no concrete motivation. It is as though the concise style at the climax of the drama does not allow such a motivation. Again we are forced to continue listening.

The section closes with the information that the king orders the arrest of 'the scribe Baruch and the prophet Jeremiah',[1] 'but YHWH hid them'. The king's destruction of the words of the prophet demands as its continuation the death of the prophet and his associate. In reality there are not two actions, but only one. But YHWH himself interferes and stops the king's plans.[2] Naturally YHWH takes the same care of Jeremiah as He took of Elijah (I Kings 17.2); at his call He had promised him to be with him and to protect him from the violence of his

---

[1] Note that the titles are mentioned in the royal order

[2] The editor of Biblia Hebraica has—just as LXX—taken offence because YHWH personally interferes on behalf of the prophet, and he suggests with LXX the reading 'and they hid themselves'. Cf. also his (Rudolph's) commentary where he hesitatingly supports the same view, and, following Duhm, calls the M.T. an 'erbauliche Wendung', which does not suit 'dem schlichten Stil Baruchs' (p. 199). This agrees with our supposition that the narrative in its present form does not derive from Baruch.

opponents (1.8). Indeed, it may be called 'edifying'; at least it is in the style of the present narrative.

If it really is an 'edifying' story it is quite clear that it cannot stop here. It would be a complete disavowal of Jeremiah and his prophecies if the king's action were to be the last word in the matter. Jeremiah's prophecy must be approved in some way or other and the intervention of YHWH, in hiding Jeremiah and Baruch, is at the same time the beginning of a new action.

As the last component part in a chiasmus the third section of the chapter follows. It is again singular to observe how the three sections at the same time are interdependent and complete in themselves. The introductory v. 27 almost recapitulates the two previous sections without destroying the style; on the contrary, just as the formula 'the word of YHWH came to Jeremiah' was accompanied in v. 1 according to the style by a more precise indication, so here too, 'after the king had burned the roll and all the words which Baruch had written at the dictation of Jeremiah'.

The king had destroyed Jeremiah's roll of prophecy and would have got rid of its authors. YHWH interfered and saved the authors. And now follows the last part: YHWH orders Jeremiah to reproduce the roll in the exact manner of the former one. Just as the intention of the king undoubtedly was to neutralize the prophecies of disaster, to avert them by destroying the roll[1] and seeking to dispatch its authors, the intention behind the reproduction of it is quite evidently to ensure that Jeremiah's prophecies remain in force. Just as the king by getting rid of the prophecy and the prophet wished to show the whole world that no mighty YHWH stood behind Jeremiah, so the consequent development shows that Jeremiah is indeed YHWH's true prophet who only speaks that which YHWH intends to do. And in the situation caused by the king's action, in this *new* situation, YHWH gives a further oracle to his prophet. So we hear an entirely new oracle against Jehoiakim, and so we are told in the last part of v. 32 'and there were added besides unto them many like words'. Every thought of

[1] Cf. too Johs. Pedersen, *Israel: its Life and Culture*, III-IV, 1940, p. 114

repentance and forgiveness disappears; all that remains is the absolute proclamation of doom for the king, for the city, and for the people he represents.

Typical of the style, and not at all unique to the book of Jeremiah is the technique we are able to trace in v. 29: here at last comes the concrete motivation for the king's behaviour, the motivation we lacked in the main section. 'Verily, the king of Babylon shall come and destroy this land and exterminate man and beast in it.' These are words that are meant as a free, concentrated rendering of the ones that provoked the wrath of Jehoiakim. A chronological account by a witness would presumably have placed v. 29 between v. 22 and v. 23,—and the narrative would no longer exist as a work of art.

As to the oracle itself there is but this to say, that with its 'rhetorical prose' it is quite parallel to the other 'Deuteronomized' Jeremiah prophecies, ch. 7, 12, 14, etc., with their characteristic idea that the prophet(s) spoke even though the people were unwilling to listen to them. This is the well-known post-exilic view of Israel's life in Canaan as a series of instances of disobedience, a period of obstinacy. It cannot be denied that this view is strongly influenced by our 'writing prophets', but it is fully developed in the historical compilation of the Deuteronomist.

We have now reached the end of the chapter and can sum up the results: Jeremiah wishes to influence the people, but is prevented. He can send another, but only by providing him with his prophecies as a credential. In accordance with Hebrew narrative technique the chapter is thus introduced by a divine command to Jeremiah to write down his prophecies on a roll. This roll, the external symbol of YHWH's threat against, and doom for, Judah constitutes the focal point of the drama. Jehoiakim destroys it to exorcize the disaster, but YHWH has Jeremiah reproduce it; the disaster looms undiminished, and is even intensified.

We will now attempt to show what the isagogical significance of the chapter is by confronting the present interpretation of the chapter with other points of view. Once again we wish to emphasize that this is a characteristic example of Hebrew narrative *art*. Neither too much nor too little is included. Our interest is spell-bound throughout the whole narrative. When commentators have scoffed at the style,[1] is not this because their demands have been foreign, and therefore irrelevant, to the situation, the time and the national character?

From the golden age of literary criticism we have Duhm's epoch-making commentary.[2] To the author's credit we note the correct conception of v. 8 as anticipating the central action. If only recent exegetes had followed Duhm in this, we should have been spared the removal of v. 9 to a position between v. 4 and v. 5, so typical of Volz's commentary,[3] and later quoted by Rudolph.[4] Otherwise we must in fact say that Duhm's reflections, revolutionary though he may be, are characteristic of his time. On v. 2 he remarks:[5] 'Jeremiah usually makes use of the spoken word, and only exceptionally does he publish his poems in a few copies; at least they are not known to the royal officials. Now YHWH inspires him to write them on a roll; in the same way Isaiah (30.8) derives his activity as an author from a command of Yahweh. He is to write down all the words of Yahweh since the time of Josiah, and this he could only do if he had already committed them to paper; the reproduction of the roll that was burned also presupposes such notes, and this agrees with the fact that the poems that are handed down to us in their original freshness reflect their date of composition, and thus cannot be improvised while being dictated for instance in the year 604.' In a like manner he comments on v. 32:[6] 'The reproduction proves that Jeremiah had dictated from written notes which he still possessed and had taken with him to his place of concealment. His involuntary leisure he uses to have all the poems written down with a view to publication.' Even though Duhm considers Jeremiah

---

[1] e.g., Duhm's commentary mentioned below, p. 291

[2] In Marti's series. It is still impossible to ignore this important work. The chapter is discussed on pp. 288-296.

[3] In Sellin's series, here quoted from 2nd ed., 1928, pp. xl f and 327 f. As a simple rearrangement of the text, placing v. 9 before v. 5, does not suffice, Volz is compelled to delete the words 'in the temple of YHWH, on a day of fast' in v. 6. The well-balanced character of v. 8 has been overlooked; and v. 10 thereby happens to contain clumsy repetitions from v. 8.

[4] In Eissfeldt's series, 1948. Cf. pp. v f and 195-201.

[5] P. 289   [6] P. 296

a prophet of the old type who regarded 'oral activity' as the essential thing, he cannot imagine the prophet managing without notes when collecting his prophecies.

The way in which ideas circulate in modern Europe is by writing and reading, and if one does not emancipate oneself from these 'cultural presuppositions' one is liable to ask with Duhm:[1] 'Was the roll only written with the purpose of being read in the Temple, or would it have been published in any case?' and one would be liable to consider the latter as the more probable.

Indeed, Duhm considers the main part of the chapter (vv. 1-26 and v. 32) to be Baruch's own description, a first class account by an eye-witness, and thinks a series of *accidents* sufficient to determine the course of events. Jeremiah is accidentally inspired to write down his prophecies, quite by accident he gets hold of a scribe Baruch, who is an adept in the necessary art of calligraphy; quite by chance Jeremiah himself is prevented from appearing in the Temple (according to Duhm because of Levitical impurity). The king's action is first of all an outcome of his lack of awe and his self-conceited nature, though one might also say that he acts as a critic and destroys what he does not like; and as he does not like anything in the roll, he destroys it all. Jeremiah uses his involuntary period of inaction, that to a certain degree was forced on him by chance, to make a collected edition of his poems in his hiding place. What one misses in Duhm, but not in him alone, is an understanding of the coherence of the chapter, the significance of events in their mutual relations.

In Volz we read[2] not only that ch. 36 gives most necessary information as to the literary-historical problem connected with the book of Jeremiah, but we are further instructed 'concerning the literary process of the prophetic writings'—which in this connection must apply to the prophetic books in general. But there are two purposes behind Jeremiah's action: both to make an impression on his contemporaries when his collected prophecies are read to them, and to preserve these speeches for later generations. For Jeremiah sees to it that the roll is

[1] P. 290 [2] P. 330

reproduced, and even adds to it.[1] The conclusion is drawn:[2] 'By using hand-bills (!!, this refers to such sections as 4.5 f, 14.1-15.3, 30 f), Jeremiah creates an intermediate form between speech and writing, and in the book he has prepared for recitation he has given an example of how he first reduced the word to writing before proclaiming it.' It seems more than singular that such a conclusion should be drawn from an account telling us that Jeremiah received a divine command after twenty-three years of activity to write down his prophecies.

When faced with a chapter such as Jer. 36 the literary critic seeks to solve two problems: the literary genesis (1) of the book of Jeremiah, and (2) of all the Scriptural prophecies. The solution of the first problem naturally entails consequences for the solution of the second. But if a satisfactory solution of the problem of the book of Jeremiah cannot be reached—and it seems doubtful whether one can be reached if the problem is to be attacked on purely literary-critical principles—is it not then still permissible to consider the events of ch. 36 typical for our scriptural prophets?

Against this we must issue a caution. With ch. 36 the book of Jeremiah apparently contains so many points of departure for an attempt at reconstructing the literary genesis of the book, that scarcely any other book in the Old Testament can compare with it. If a favourable solution is not reached on this basis, it must either be because the literary critical method is insufficient, perhaps inadequate, or because the literary activity described in ch. 36 has its special aims and only serves the interests of the moment,—or perhaps both reasons contribute to the failure of the attempt.

But has the attempt failed? We need only quote what the literary critic Volz remarks about Mowinckel's *Zur Komposition des Buches Jeremias*, published in 1914, and as is well-known one of the most radical attempts in modern times to reconstruct the literary genesis of the book in all its phases. Among other

---

[1] However, on p. 334 another motivation (?) is given for the reproduction of the roll: the words of YHWH cannot be burned or destroyed by any enemy
[2] P. xli

things Volz writes:[1] 'Even repeated examination cannot make me accept this view . . . I wonder if we shall ever be able to reconstruct the genesis of the book of Jeremiah in all its details as Mowinckel would like?' We prefer to put it thus: Even though Jer. 36 is a gold mine for the literary scholar who seeks for light as to the genesis of the book, the material in the rest of the book of Jeremiah is too contradictory. We can illustrate this by reminding the reader of Mowinckel's latest attempt at a solution.[2]

Mowinckel is greatly occupied with Baruch's book (the reproduced roll with later additions; cf. v. 32) and says the roll was in Baruch's possession; would it not then naturally be he who began to add other words, i.e., traditions of and about his friend Jeremiah? He finds this confirmed by the fact that the book concludes with a word to Baruch (ch. 45),[3] a word, that chronologically belongs together with ch. 36, and that for other reasons as well must have obtained this pre-eminent position. For it is meant as the signature of the author, 'the indirect presentation of the author to the reader'.[4] In other words we can trace a book of Baruch from ch. 1-45. But in this book there is yet more: a whole series of prose speeches, imbued with the Deuteronomistic spirit and composed in Deuteronomistic language. It is not here a question of a special source, but of speeches representing a quite definite school of tradition where certain words of Jeremiah have been transmitted and changed according to the thoughts and the style, dominant in the school.[5] It is an open question how these speeches were incorporated into Baruch's book. Was Baruch's book subjected to further oral tradition, or are the speeches literary insertions?

[1] *Op. cit.*, p. xliii, n. 1   [2] Cf. *Prophecy and Tradition*, pp. 21 f and 61 ff
[3] Chs. 46-51 and 52 are independent complexes, added at a later date
[4] P. 62
[5] It is strange that Mowinckel should exclaim here: 'In this case—and it is of interest to stress this in order to modify Nyberg's and Engnell's views of the fixity of verbal tradition—it is the written form, Baruch's recordings, which have best preserved the original; the oral parallel tradition is in this definite case "a further development" and a transformation of the original Jeremiah saying' (*op. cit.*, p. 22). Why is it of interest to stress this *in this definite case*? How should a view be thereby modified that maintains the general reliability of oral tradition to the same degree as written? Here, in this definite case, we have to do with a circle of tradition with its own character, quite definite and quite independent of the master.

In view of ch. 3 where metrically composed words (vv. 1-5, 12b-13, 19-20) are interrupted by prose passages (vv. 6-12a, 14-18), Mowinckel thinks he is able to establish that it at any rate seems to be certain that the speeches were inserted in an already existing book.[1] The way in which the prose passages as well as the 'Baruch text' are divided and combined in ch. 3 would seem to indicate, that they both—i.e. the Deuteronomized speeches as well—existed in written form before they were combined.

However, as early as 1938 Birkeland[2] drew attention to ch. 25.1-13. He rightly considers the last words in v. 13 'which Jeremiah prophesied against all the nations', a superscription to 25.15-38, and considers vv. 1-13ba the evident conclusion of a book. Strangely enough these concluding words are composed—not in the metrical form so familiar from the 'book of Baruch', but in prose style and with Deuteronomistic phrases (v. 3, cf. 36.31; 11.8; 13.10, etc.; v. 4, cf. 7.13; 7.25, etc.). But if the Deuteronomistic passages in the book of Baruch had been inserted by a purely literary process we should expect that the original conclusion of the book (i.e. the original roll) would have been preserved verbatim. As this is not the case there can hardly be any doubt that the 'book' has been subjected to further oral transmission, and this confirms the view that we have formed on ch. 36: that special conditions led to the writing down of Jeremiah's prophecies, conditions so special that the book, as the *novum* it was, was not able to break the prevalent method of tradition.

If one accepts the reliability of oral tradition (and Mowinckel does, when on one hand he says of the book of Baruch that it certainly was the first prophetic book in existence,[3] and on the other hand considers it possible to establish the genuine words of Hosea and Amos), one can form another picture of the composition of the book of Jeremiah, a picture that, it is to

---

[1] P. 64   [2] *Zum hebräischen Traditionswesen*, 1938, pp. 44 ff
[3] A statement that might be questioned on serious grounds. The prophecy of Nahum is definitely called in its superscription *sēpher Nahūm*, the *book* of Nahum, and according to recent research (cf., e.g., Bentzen, *Introduction*, 2nd ed., 1952, vol. ii, p. 149) the date of this book has to be placed in all probability between 626 and 612 B.C., several years before the events related in Jer. 36.

be hoped, will prove to coincide with the technique of Deuteronomistic circles as a whole.

We know the mode of procedure in these circles from the Deuteronomic historical compilation as well as from Deuteronomy itself. Early legal provisions appear in Deuteronomy with comments in a diffuse prose style; only in a few cases is it possible to surmise that the original wording of the old law is still preserved (cf. Deut. 14.22 and 14.23 f); usually the whole passage is composed in the same style. The fact that ancient law material is being used, is shown by a comparison with the book of the Covenant. In the Deuteronomic historical compilation we again find old and new material. In some places we are introduced to old traditions that only harmonize poorly with the tendency of the work; they are neutralized by Deuteronomistic contributions, but they *are* mentioned at any rate (cf. I Sam. 8-12). In other places legendary material about the prophets is subjected to a thoroughly artistic and tendentious revision; we may mention the chapters on Elijah (I Kings 17 ff), which in their construction have become a part of the historical compilation itself to such a degree that the 'exposition' has been given in the usual religious evaluation accompanying the chronological-genealogical notices (I Kings 17.29 ff). Behind that tradition one cannot—at any rate by literary critical methods—trace the original prophetic legend, although a comparison with the Elisha stories shows how radical the Deuteronomistic treatment of Elijah has been.

And now the book of Jeremiah. Here we have words in metrical form as well as prose speeches based on words of Jeremiah. It is impossible that the Temple speech (cf. Jer. 26) should have been lacking in the original roll; nonetheless we look for it in vain in its original wording and must be content with Jer. 7, which is, and remains, a prose text in spite of all attempts so far to prove anything to the contrary; to be sure it is rhetorical prose, i.e. of just the kind that is characteristic of the Deuteronomists. If the present book of Jeremiah had been composed in the manner sketched by Mowinckel, one would have to assume that one of the most important words of Jeremiah had been excised. In our opinion the 'Deuteronomists', to whom we owe the Deuteronomistic historical compilation and the book of Jeremiah, in fact give us examples of their mode of treating tradition, now reproducing it verbatim, now duplicating tradition, now completely revising it. It is therefore not the oral tradition as such which has given us passages such as Jer. 3.6-11 and 3.14-18 or ch. 7. A conscious revision has taken place, presumably because the Deuteronomists were specially interested in certain points.

We have examined a modern attempt by literary criticism to solve the riddle of the book of Jeremiah, an attempt which in our opinion failed to master the refractory material by employing literary critical methods. We have made the remark above that the circumstances of Jer. 36 were quite peculiar. We will examine this once again a little more closely.

As against the assertion by the great majority of scholars (Volz, Birkeland, Bentzen, Mowinckel) that the form 'nōsaph' in v. 32 should be interpreted as referring to later additions, and that the sentence represents the point of view of the later editor—the Niph'al form is supposed to imply all this—and the use of this interpretation to reconstruct, with more or less precision and in greater or less detail, a history of the development of the book of Jeremiah, we must maintain that that book and its chapter 36 are not in reality a solid foundation for such far-reaching constructions. Widengren is, in fact, quite right in maintaining[1] that it is a baseless and unproved assertion that 'nōsaph' means 'later additions', i.e. additions by others. The sentence in question must no doubt be regarded as a circumstantial clause describing in more detail the conditions under which the roll was reproduced.[2] Had it been a question of the favourite form of the literary critics, one would have expected a clarifying ''ahar' or the like, but the search for any such thing is in vain both in M.T. and in LXX. And so the basis for the search for 'Urrolle und Nachtrag'[3] collapses. If our views on Jer. 36 hold good, it will be evident that the light that this chapter throws on the literary genesis of the scriptural prophecy as a whole is very small indeed.

[1] *Op. cit.*, p. 72, n. 4
[2] Cf. our exegesis above
[3] To use Eissfeldt's terminology; cf. his *Einleitung*, pp. 393 ff

We may conclude by indicating a problem. The Deuteronomic historical work culminates in the finding of a book; according to the account in Deuteronomy, but in contrast to that in the book of Chronicles, this book occasioned a series of reforms already in the days of the Judaean kings. The Deuteronomistic book of Jeremiah contains in a prominent position an account of a prophetic book that was read aloud to the devout king's son. We have already had occasion to find a plain allusion to II Kings 22 by virtue of contrast. In our opinion it appears to be established that Deuteronomy as we know it can by no means be a pre-exilic book. And this is still more evident with regard to the book of Jeremiah. However, it was presumably no random guess that caused Deuteronomy to be identified with Josiah's law-book. On the contrary, this was just what the author(s) of the Deuteronomic historical compilation wished every reader to do.[1] The question is whether in our chapter a like motive has asserted itself with regard to the book of Jeremiah, not the book of Jeremiah as it is now, but a work of Jeremiah that at one time or another— presumably during the exile—was composed by these circles, a work ending with these words: 'And this whole land shall become a desolation and a wilderness, and these nations shall serve the king of Babylon seventy years. And when the seventy years are accomplished, then will I punish the king of Babylon and this nation, says YHWH, for their iniquities, and also the land of the Chaldeans (will I punish), and I will make it a perpetual desolation. And I will bring upon that land all my words, which I have pronounced against it, even all that is written in this book' (25.11-13*ba*).

Micah 4-5

From the following criticism and analysis it will, I hope, appear that the *literary critical* work on the prophetic books evidently pursues a double aim. On one hand an attempt is made to find the very words of the prophet in question; these

---

[1] This becomes especially evident when we—following Noth and Engnell— restrict the designation: 'Deuteronomic historical work' so that it only applies to Deut.—II Kings

must naturally never be identified in advance with the book we know by the prophet's name. On the other hand it is attempted to explain through what phases the original collection of prophetic oracles passed in order to become our present prophetic book. By means of certain established criteria a portion of the material is separated from the rest as being secondary. An attempt is made to determine the age of this secondary material, and by this means it is believed to be possible to reconstruct, with more or less accuracy, the development of the prophetic book in question often through a period of several centuries. The literary and historical investigations go hand in hand; a separation of them is impossible. The heart of the work is the effort to recover the prophet's own book, to get back to his original message without the later additions. In order to do this the necessary prerequisite is, as likewise appears in the purest literary criticism, that the reduction to writing of a saying is contemporaneous with the origin of the saying. Not the spoken word, but the written word can be preserved intact throughout the ages.

The *traditio-historian* proceeds in a different way. He attempts to distinguish between the historical and the literary aspect of the investigation, and he first devotes himself to the literary investigation. In this way the complex of tradition with which he is concerned is first of all separated from its surroundings, and then an understanding of its structure is attempted. The passages having a literary relation are defined, the central point of the complex is sought for, and an attempt is made to explore the possibility of understanding the remaining material as literary deposits around this nucleus. Supported by the knowledge available from other sources as to the conditions for oral composition and oral transmission, the scholar tries to describe how this *literary* deposit around a nucleus can have taken place, and why a nucleus has attracted precisely that material by which it is at present surrounded. But this does not yet prove anything as to the historical value of the different sayings, their value as a source of information as to the prophet's message. This is an entirely different problem, the solution of which can only be attempted when the literary investigation is brought to an end. It is a matter of opinion whether the traditio-historian's historical investigations—if he embarks upon them at all—should commence with the nucleus or with the deposits. Personally we think it most natural to commence with the nucleus. If this nucleus can without contradiction be fitted into the historical pattern, from which tradition asserts that it derives, there is scarcely reason to doubt the correctness of the tradition. But certainty is something we never attain. If the deposits exhibit more than a formal relationship with the nucleus, or exhibit an inherent relationship with it in spite of formal differences, and even in spite of apparent or perhaps demonstrable differences, then we can plead the authenticity of these sayings, in the first case in full measure, in the second in a substantial measure. If the lack of inner relationship is felt too strongly, it is naturally necessary to emphasize the role of tradition for these deposits, which thus testify to a later revision, perhaps a modification, of the thoughts of the prophet. But even in this case these passages retain considerable value—in principle, however, neither greater nor less value than the supposedly original sayings of the prophet. Of course there are people who apotheosize the prophets. For them the 'secondary' is equivalent to the inferior. For the historian who can date these deposits, they become however useful illustrations of the views held in certain times and in certain circles on certain matters.

As the pursuit of the prophet's own words is an essential concern of literary criticism in its radical as well as its conservative form, we have first of all to examine the complex, Mic. 4-5, in its relation to the remainder of the book of Micah, among other reasons because radical criticism in its classical form as it appears in Karl Marti's commentary[1] does not recognize any authentic saying by Micah after Mic. 3.12. Marti's argument is briefly this: Jer. 26.18, which quotes Mic.3.12, shows that a hundred years after the prophet's activity he was still remembered as a great and bold, but remorseless, prophet of doom. And this is just the picture of him we know from Mic. 1-3 (without their secondary additions); this section is a compact

---

[1] *Dodekapropheton* (Kurzer Hand-Commentar), 1904, pp. 258-302

composition which gives us a non-contradictory picture of the prophet of doom. And it is precisely this section that closes with the oracle of doom against Zion quoted in Jer. 26.18. If Micah had spoken sanguinely, if he had promised the people that they should not only be saved, but live in happiness and prosperity, it would have taken the sting out of his prophecy of doom, and he would not have been remembered as in Jer. 26.18. Mic. 4-7 is, however, largely composed of promises and words of consolation, and these must therefore be weeded out as secondary additions; Marti even considers it possible to ascribe them to exilic, post-exilic, nay, even Maccabaean times. On the same grounds he has rejected vv. 12-13 from ch. 2, vv. 2-4 from ch. 1, and based on wholly untenable criteria 1.10-15. The remainder of 1-3 is then an authentic writing of Micahs deriving from the prophet himself.[1] The following chapter, of Micah are gathered around two crystallization points, (1) the promise to Zion, and (2) the requirements for true worship of God, 4.1-4 and 6.6-8 respectively. The humane and ethical spirit of these two sayings is so close to that of Micah[2] that they may be considered as the earliest additions to the book of Micah. Then 4.5 is placed between 4.4 and 6.6 as a connecting link. The connection is, however, lost when in the second century some eschatological material is inserted; because of this 6.6 ff is furnished with a new introduction 6.1-4a, and this in its turn brings new threats with it, 6.9-7.6. But as the book was to end on an optimistic note, the two psalms 7.8-20 (from the second century) were added. Marti gives Mic. 4-5 the superscription: the salvation in the time of the Messiah; the two chapters are a conglomeration, the oldest elements of of which, 4.1-4 and 5.2 and 5.4, date from about 500 B.C.,

---

[1] He has written it down himself, 'for, in the first place, the trend of thought in chaps. 1-3 is irreproachable when the foreign matter is excised, and the rounding off of the whole with 3.12, which refers back to 1.5b, is quite evident, so that it is better to ascribe the arrangement to the author than to a later compiler. Secondly, Micah might just as well as Isaiah feel himself forced to write down his words as a testimony to the future after Jerusalem had been saved, an event that to him must have seemed a mere delay of the fulfilment of his prophecy. And finally the writings of Hosea and Amos must have existed, so it was a matter of course that Micah too wrote down his words.'

[2] According to Marti they belong to the sixth or fifth centuries, and are thus separated from Micah by about two hundred years!

while the latest, 5.5-15, indicates a time near the second century, and the remainder must be ascribed to some period after Ezekiel. Naturally in this survey by Marti of the origin of the book of Micah the exegetical results of the commentary itself are anticipated. But the central point in the argument, the comparison of Mic. 3.12 with Jer. 26.18 and the consequences derived from this, do not presuppose any careful, detailed exegesis of the whole book of Micah. This result can be obtained quite simply by insisting on two things: (1) that Jeremiah's contemporaries by reading Micah's own *book* could see that Micah was an inexorable prophet of doom, and (2) the fact that the climax of this book, 3.12, is quoted, since as a climax it could not be weakened by anything following, and therefore is best placed at the end. Indisputably one receives the impression that the aim of Marti's exegetical work is (1) to ascribe a late date to everything in the book of Micah after 3.12, and (2) by various excisions to make of ch. 1-3 an ideal book, rounded off and with an 'irreproachable' progress of thought.

How forceful this argument—which Marti shares with his contemporaries as well as with his teachers, particularly Stade —is, may be seen for instance from G. Hylmö's *Kompositionen av Mikas Bok*, 1919. He is not so radical in his criticism as Marti but assumes for instance that the basic elements in Mic. 4-5, i.e., Mic. 4.1-4, 9, 10*a*; 5.2, 10, 11, 12, 13*a*, 14*b*, derive from Micah himself. But, Hylmö says, these verses do not belong to the collection of oracles, ch. 1-3, compiled by Micah himself. His friends and adherents have preserved them—perhaps these fragments went by his name—but they were only added to the book of Micah after 586 B.C., that is, some time after the episode in Jer. 26.18. As the treatment of Mic. 4-5 by the purely literary critical method has nowhere been attempted in so detailed a manner as by Hylmö,[1] we can refer those who wish for a thorough account of the view of literary criticism on the genesis of Mic. 4 f to this book, which appraises the most important critical research up to 1919. We are prevented by lack of space from a more detailed discussion of it. This

[1] *Op. cit.*, pp. 95-252. Cf. further pp. 286-88.

chapter should be more than a polemic against views that have long since been given up. We can only say that a closer study of it has convinced us how dominant the 'book-view' was in the age of literary criticism and how disastrous it was to the understanding of the structure of the books of the prophets. In this case Micah wrote a book, 1-3. A detailed exegesis of Mic. 4-7 shows that some few sayings here may quite likely go back to Micah himself. The conclusion has been stated above.[1]

For the time being let us ignore the attempts of recent research to stress the oral nature of ancient civilizations and ask: Is it *likely* that a prophetical book originated according to the principles laid down by Marti and others? Is it likely that from the time of the exile until the time of the Maccabees the extant prophetical writings were re-edited at intervals, and the message of these writings adapted time and again to the needs of successive generations? Is it likely considering the literary critics' own suppositions? We think not. According to the literary critics[2] the prophets' mode of action was to publish their oracles in written form, first perhaps in the form of hand-bills, then in collections of oracles compiled by themselves or their disciples. But publication implies multiplication. How then is one to imagine that the later additions were affixed? If one man began to add something, then a hundred others could protest and accuse such an editor of falsification and produce proofs, in black and white. Or are we to believe that at various times editorial committees were convened and perhaps by a vote of a majority resolved to incorporate an oracle of dubious origin in one prophetical book or another? Or perhaps only a single copy of each prophetical writing was preserved till post-exilic times so that the editors had a free hand? As far as I know, the interminable discussions as to whether such and such a verse belongs to such and such a prophet do not belong to late Judaism but to the close of the nineteenth century A.D. Would it not be advisable to ignore the 'book-view' a moment?

Instead of the literary critical method we will now try the traditio-historical one, not primarily to demonstrate that it is

---

[1] It is found in Hylmö, *op. cit.*, pp. 212 and 286 ff
[2] Please excuse the generalization!

more capable of solving the problems, but in order to point out the difference between it and that of the literary critics. We will first discuss whether it is justifiable to delimit chs. 4-5 as an independent complex of tradition as against 1-3 and 6-7. As to the delimitation of 4-5 as against 1-3 it is immediately evident that while 1-3 largely consist of didactic revelations and maledictions,[1] chs. 4-5 are mainly a series of sayings concerning the future, proclaiming 'what is to happen', 'in the last days' and 'on that day'. In 6.1 a new didactic revelation begins, related to 1.2 ff in form as well as in content. And so there is good reason to consider 4-5 an independent complex of tradition. The content of this complex is as follows: 4.1-4 is a promise of the exaltation of Zion in the last days, when nations shall flock to Zion to acquire knowledge of YHWH's ways, and the peace of God shall reign everywhere; 4.5 says that when all others walk in the name of their God, then will we walk in the name of our God; 4.6-8 declares that the remnant that is halt and has been driven out shall be gathered together and become a strong nation, YHWH shall be their king, and to Zion, 'the tower of the shepherd', the former dominion shall return; 4.9-5.6, the central portion of the complex, can be divided into several lesser units, 4.9-10, 4.11-13, 5.1, that have this in common that they are all concerned with the immediate distress of the daughter of Zion, and 5.2-6, which proclaims the birth of the descendant of David and the deliverance from the Assyrians, a turning point which is reached when 'the remnant of his brethren shall turn to the children of Israel'; 5.7-9 contains two sayings about the remnant of Jacob, to which is added an exhortation that 'thy hand shall be lifted up against thy adversaries'; 5.10-15 announces that on that day horses, chariots, and strongholds shall be destroyed, together with every kind of idolatry, and that YHWH will execute vengeance upon the disobedient.

If we examine this subject-matter more closely we discover a curious relationship between its units, two and two. (*a*) 4.1-4 speaks of the exaltation of Zion, of the dominating position of this mountain of God among the nations as a religious centre

---

[1] Introduced by 'shime'û' 1.2; 3.1; 3.9, and 'hôy' 2.1

where people can really learn the ways of YHWH, for 'instruction goes forth from Zion, and the word of YHWH from Jerusalem'; 5.10-15 deals with the abolition of false worship, witchcraft and soothsaying, idols and 'maṣṣēbāhs,' together with 'ashērāhs'. To the words about the extirpation of the entire military power in 5.10 f corresponds the description of 4.3 f of how in the last days swords shall be hammered into plough-shares and lances into pruning-hooks, and of how men shall learn war no more, but every man shall sit under his vine and under his fig-tree, and none shall make him afraid. The complex is thus neatly framed by two sayings with related contents. (*b*) From this 'universalism' 4.5 paves the way to more nationally emphasized sayings about the remnant, 5.7 f and 9, declaring that the halt and the outcast shall be assembled and made a remnant, a strong nation over whom YHWH shall reign for ever on Zion. 'And unto thee, O tower of the shepherd, hill of the daughter of Zion, unto thee shall it come, even the former dominion, the kingdom of the daughter of Jerusalem.' But 5.7 f and 9 also speak of the 'remnant', 'she'ērīth Yaʻakōbh', which shall be among the peoples as a dew from YHWH, independent of men's expectations, as a lion from whose clutches none can deliver the prey. The nation that now is weak and hard pressed by enemies shall become independent and mighty. (*c*) As will be seen, we have gradually approached the central section, the negative portions of which are formed by the passages on the present distress of the daughter of Zion, 4.9-5.1, while the positive portion consists of the promise about Bethlehem, the proclamation of the appearance of a ruler who shall be a strong bulwark against the enemy, Assyria. As far as we know, nobody has in recent times drawn attention to the curious structure of this complex with a nucleus consisting of negative and positive elements, i.e. its prophecies of misfortune and good fortune, and its surrounding layers; the first of these, 4.6-8 and 5.7-9, consists of promises to the remnant, and around this is a layer, 4.1-4, of promises of a purified and glorious worship, a time of peace, in which Zion is to be the centre, and finally of a time in which the people are deprived of their false images, the weapons and the cult of Canaan,

5.10-15. Even though the parallel passages are related they are far from identical, and we will not for the time being give any opinion as to whether they are derived from the same man, perhaps from the prophet Micah himself. We have already suggested that the passages belong to different categories by dividing them into three groups and by designating 4.5 a bridge between 'universalism' and 'nationalism'.

But if these passages belong to relatively different categories how are we to explain that they have been linked together in this complex of tradition? We emphasize once again that we are attempting to explain the matter by the traditio-historical method, and not historically, by suggesting, for instance, that it might be Micah himself or some unknown men from the days of the exile, etc., who were the compilers of this composition. Let us examine the nucleus of this complex a little more closely in order to find in it the solution of the riddle of this composition. As the 'layers' are largely of a positive nature, it will be advisable to seek the solution in the positive part of the nucleus, Mic. 5.2-6.

This prophecy about Bethlehem, so hotly debated in recent times,[1] is characterized by the following: (1) a combination of mythological and historical allusions in the promise of a coming ruler, so that the prophecy may be regarded as parallel to the 'Immanuel-promise';[2] (2) the mention of a certain period that must elapse before the saviour king will come bringing victory and good fortune; (3) the mention of the historical enemy from whom the people is to be saved. In (2) and (3) our oracle is again related to the 'Immanuel prophecy'.

Important for the understanding of the structure of Mic. 4-5

[1] See for instance Hylmö, ad loc. pp. 192 ff. Hylmö assumes, *inter alia* on the basis of rhythmical criteria, pp. 202 f, that v. 2 is genuine an oracle that with the prominence it gives to Beth-Ephratah is supposed to agree with Micah's condemnation of the metropolis, Jerusalem (208). That vv. 3-4 may belong to a much later date may, according to Hylmö 'hardly be denied by any modern scholar' (p. 198). Fortunately fashion changes from time to time. A criterion for the ascription of a late date is sought in the 'common supposition' that the verses play on the Immanuel prophecy and the name of Isaiah's son Shear-jashub. For it is a custom belonging to later times that on the basis of older prophecies calculations are made as to the time and hour for the coming of the kingdom of glory (pp. 199 f)—as though there really was any 'calculation' in this pregnant sentence: 'until the remnant of his brethren return to the children of Israel'.

[2] See Hammershaimb in *Studia Theologica*, III, (1949), 1951, p. 138

is the fact that the mention of the interval of time in Mic. 5.2 contains an element that can explain why the 'remnant passages', Mic. 4.6-8 and 5.7-9, were deposited around the Bethlehem prophecy. For 5.3 says: 'Therefore will he [YHWH] give them [the people] up, until the time when she who travails has brought forth, and the *remnant of his* [the people's] *brethren shall return unto the children of Israel.*' The language is obscure, the suffixes seem to have no relation to the previous passage: 'from thee unto me shall come forth one who is to be the ruler of Israel, and his going forth shall be from of old, from the days of long ago'.[1] If one reflects upon the situation behind the oracle, the interpretation indicated by the parentheses above becomes the only one possible. But what is really meant by the expression 'the remnant of his brethren', and what does it mean that 'they shall return to the children of Israel'? Since the people to whom a ruler is promised in v. 2 is Judah, the remnant of his brethren must mean the remnant of Judah's brethren. That this refers to the Northern Israelites is evident from the fact that the passage continues 'they shall return'. For an exhortation 'to return', or a prophecy that so-and-so 'shall return', must be directed at the apostates (cf. Amos 4.6 ff; Hos. 6.1, 2.9). And that view was held in Judaean, or what amounts to the same thing, Jerusalemite circles, where it was held that the political and cultural emancipation of the northern kingdom after the reign of Solomon was tantamount to apostasy. This is evident from Isa. 7.17, *inter alia*, with its mention of 'Ephraim's departure from Judah', 'sūr mē'al', for this is one of the terms most commonly applied to religious apostasy.[2] How does this agree with the statement that 'the remnant of his brethren shall return to the children of *Israel*'? Apparently not at all, for 'Israel' appears to have been used of the northern kingdom or the northern tribes, as opposed to the tribe of Judah, in several texts, some of which are very

---

[1] The expression: 'mōṣā'ōthāw mikkedhem' is equally 'historical' and 'mythological'; cf. the use of 'yāṣā" of the going forth of the celestial bodies on their courses, Ps. 19.5 (the sun, YHWH), and the Accadian Shamash, cf. *K.B.*, VI, i, 98, l.47: '-ṣi- tuk-ka ip-ḫu-ru ilāni māti' = 'at thy going forth the gods of the country assemble'

[2] See G.-B., 17th ed., p. 539, s.v. 'sūr', c

ancient.[1] But this objection carries little weight when we consider that the old Israelite sacred object, the Ark of the Covenant, which had stood in Jerusalem since the time of David cast an *Israelite* nimbus around this ancient Canaanite holy place. In reality it is against this background that it is possible for those in Judah and Jerusalem to speak of the Northerners' apostasy, i.e., an apostasy from Zion and the Ark of the Covenant on which YHWH Sabaoth sat enthroned.

Thus there is this connecting element between the central portion of Mic. 4-5 and the sayings of 4.6 ff and 5.7 ff, which mention the remnant. Now it is evident that the remnant in 5.3 must mean the Northern Israelites, perhaps those that were led into captivity in the years between 734 and 720 B.C., or perhaps those that remained behind. As to the sections concerning the remnant in the book of Micah it has been maintained in the last sixty-five years that they date from exilic or post-exilic times and are concerned with the Jewish 'gōlāh' in Babylon.[2] Only Ryssel urged in 1887[3] that there was indeed an exile before the Babylonian one. But suppose we take as a working hypothesis, either that the 'remnant' passages originally referred to the Northern Israelites after the fall of Samaria, or that the circles which have transmitted the Micah prophecies to us and are responsible for Mic. 4-5 in its present form understood the 'remnant prophecies' as referring to the Northern Israelites. 'I shall assemble the halt, and the outcast I shall gather together and that which I have afflicted. And that which is halt I shall make a remnant, and that which had been led to the other side (?; LXX has a different reading) a strong people, and YHWH shall be king over them on mount Zion from henceforth, even for ever.'[4] The lexicographical[5] objections raised against the

---

[1] II Sam. 2.9 and 17; 19.41 and 20.1

[2] An exception is Sellin's highly artificial interpretation on the basis of Jer. 4.5 and 8.14, in *Das Zwölfprophetenbuch*, 1922, pp. 275 f, 283 f, 291 f

[3] *Untersuchungen über die Textgestalt und die Echtheit des Buches Michas*, p. 216, here quoted from Hylmö, *op. cit.*, p. 68 (comment on 2.12-13)

[4] Mic. 4.6-7

[5] 'The halt' (haṣṣōlēʿāh) and 'the outcast' (hanniddāḥāh) from Zeph. 3.19 on are used of the Judaeans. Cf., however, Jer. 30.17 (of northern Israel): 'For "the outcast" they named you . . .' That these terms were later used of the captive Judaeans cannot prove that they were not originally used of those led into captivity from the northern kingdom.

interpretation of 4.6-7 of the Northern Israelites are of lesser significance than the fact that the express prominence given to the reign of YHWH *on Zion* fits hand in glove with the Jerusalem-ite demand for monopoly, as expressed in Mic. 5.3. And what is more, 5.9 can be joined organically to 4.6-7, for 'the former dominion' is then taken to mean, not as is usually assumed the kingdom of Judah before the exile, but the Davidic-Solomonic era, i.e., just that era which is the background for the promise of the new David who shall be ruler in Israel (5.2).[1] And if it is possible to understand 4.6-8 as indicated above, the same is naturally true of the sayings about 'the remnant of Jacob'[2] immediately following the Bethlehem prophecy, 5.7 ff.

It remains for us to discuss how Mic. 4.1-4 and 5.10-15 fit into this connection.[3] Let us first consider Hylmö's attempt to 'save' Mic. 5.2, by the argument that the same Micah who in 3.12 threatened Jerusalem with complete destruction and generally spoke of the depravity that issued from the large cities and their aristocracy, and who himself came from the country, might have spoken of salvation as something proceeding from the small provincial town, 5.2. To this we must remark, that, to be sure, it was never forgotten in Israel and Judah that David *came* from Bethlehem. And that is just why Bethlehem is mentioned in connection with the hoped-for *coming* of the new David. But David is not remembered especially because he was born in Bethlehem, but because he created a mighty kingdom and founded a dynasty in connection with the residential city which he conquered and which therefore came to bear his name. This city, Jerusalem, he made the cultic centre of the kingdom at the same time that he took over and transferred to his own person its sacred traditions. So

[1] A linguistic argument for the late origin of 5.9 has been found in the verb ''āthāh', which is supposed to be an Aramaism, i.e. taken over from the spoken language in post-exilic times. But the verb occurs in old texts such as Deut. 33.2 and Ps. 68.31. And the introductory phrase 'And thou', 'we'attāh', may be taken to indicate that we are at a focal point; cf. the exactly parallel 5.2.

[2] 'Jacob' in 3.1 and 3.9 does as a matter of fact mean Judaeans; cf. above, p. 88. on Israel. But in 1.5 it is plainly used of the northern Israelites.

[3] Lack of space prevents us from discussing 4.9-5.1 in detail. Many things indicate that at least 4.10b represents a later addition; vv. 11-13 do not seem to be of quite the same nature as vv. 9 f and 5.1, but have the picture of the distress of Zion in common with them.

firmly did he attach his name to this city that it is quite vain to try to separate him and his dynasty from it. The promise of a new David is *eo ipso* a promise of new glory for Zion, a promise of 'the former dominion' when Zion stands as the centre of the nations, and its ruler with the full authority of YHWH as guarantor of righteousness, peace and happiness. It is this theology that finds expression in Pss. 2, 18, 19, 76 and 78, etc. A theology of this nature which tends to glorify the place of the cult as God's own place and maintains its superiority to every other cultic place, is hardly the product of historical developments known to us, but timeless in itself. In *Israelite* literature the conception of the exaltation of *Zion* may therefore be as old as the Davidic dynasty.

While we sought the connecting link for the 'remnant passages' Mic. 4.9-5.6 in Mic. 5.3, the return of the remnant to Israel, the connecting link between Mic. 4.1-4 and 5.10-15 is Mic. 5.4: 'And he shall stand forth and watch in the strength of YHWH, in the majesty of the name of YHWH, his God, and they shall abide (in safety), for then he shall be great unto the ends of the earth.'

We have thus shown that Mic. 4-5 is a complex of traditions with a nucleus of which especially the negative portions evince a concrete historical situation behind the promise; and the further we depart from the nucleus, the more ideological does the nature of this promise become. Let us now consider whether anything in this complex can explain why it has been placed beween Mic. 3.12 and 6.1. Once again we emphasize that to begin with we will ignore the question of authorship, i.e., a solution reached by the aid of history. Even though one might successfully establish the thesis that Mic. 4-5 originated from another and perhaps a later hand than that of the author of Mic. 1-3, one would still have to try to find the motive that made someone or other place these two collections of oracles together.

It is not the *similarity* that caused 3.9-12 to be succeeded by 4.1-4, for seemingly one cannot imagine any greater contrast. The one section speaks of violence and injustice in Zion, of bribery and false prophecies coupled with the superstitious belief of the inhabitants of Jerusalem that Zion cannot perish, and for this reason it threatens that 'for your sakes' Zion shall be ploughed like a field, and the Temple shall become a 'bāmāh-sanctuary'.[1] On the other hand the following section announces the coming glory of Zion, Zion's exaltation above all the hills, the thronging of the nations to Zion to learn of the ways of YHWH, Zion as the place from which justice shall go forth through the whole world so that men can hammer their weapons into plough-shares and quite forget the art of war. The only thing the two passages have in common is in reality the mention of Zion. But perhaps that is not such a very insignificant feature after all. For no matter whether one turns from 4.1-4 to 3.9-12 or from 3.9-12 to 4.1-4 it is impossible to help noticing, if one compares the two passages at all carefully, that the contrast is carried out in detail. The ploughing of Zion and the exaltation of Zion; Zion as a jungle sanctuary and Zion exalted above the hills; Zion built in violence and blood-shed and Zion as the place from which YHWH's word and teaching goes forth, from which the nations shall be judged; Zion shall become heaps and the nations shall come to Zion with peaceful intentions. The thought forces itself upon us that these passages cannot even have originated independently of each other. For the present we can leave it to the historians and the psychologists to decide whether it is impossible that the same man can say that Zion because of its corruption by the conduct of the princes shall be razed to the ground *on their account*, and at the same time promise that Zion shall be exalted in the last days. We think that one ought to be cautious in postulating psychological and historical impossibilities.[2] But as a traditio-historian one is obliged to consider another question. Mic. 4.1-3 is found almost word for word in Isa. 2.2-4. The four possible solutions of the problem we are faced with are: (1) the oracle is older than both Isaiah and Micah;

[1] Cf. Hans Schmidt's interpretation ad loc. (*Die grossen Propheten* (S.A.T. II ii), 1923, pp. 136 f)
[2] In the cult one experiences not only the triumph of the powers of Chaos but also the re-creation of the community by YHWH's victory. Mic. 3.10, loosely joined to the passage as it is, is perhaps a strophe of cultic-ideological nature, cf. Hab. 2.12.

(2) Micah has the priority; (3) Isaiah is the author; (4) the oracle is of later date and interpolated in Micah as well as Isaiah. In recent times the weight of opinion lies with (3) or (4).[1] We wish to warn against a too literary view of the matter. In the form the oracle has in Micah it is (*a*) a direct and complete contrast to Mic. 3.9-12, (*b*) not without elements connecting it with Mic. 5.2 ff. On the other hand interpreters of Isaiah have not been unwilling to recognize an inner relationship between Isa. 2.2-4 and those oracles which are indubitably attributed to Isaiah. At the same time it should be noted that the majority of interpreters maintain that the oracle exists in its original form in Isaiah's *younger* contemporary Micah. The verse corresponding to Mic. 4.4 is lacking in Isaiah. That is to say that one of them can hardly have borrowed it from the other, and many things would seem to indicate that it is not wholly out of place in either Isaiah or Micah. Above we have established the indeterminable age of such oracles, and if such oracles are conceivable in Israel after the instalment of the Davidic dynasty on Zion, we think it most natural to regard Mic. 4.1-4 and Isa. 2.2-4 as an older oracle, the platform, so to speak, of the Zionism of that age. And then it is admissible to draw an *historical* conclusion. Both prophets pronounce judgement on Jerusalem, and in both prophetic books we find expressions for the might of Zion. If the oracle is older than Micah and Isaiah it is also, as the complete contrast to Mic. 3.9-12, a direct basis of this generally recognized, and in the Old Testament well-attested, oracle by Micah about the sin and destruction of Jerusalem. At any rate it is no accident that Mic. 1-3 is followed by Mic. 4-5.

Genesis 6-9

Turning now to the narrative literature of the Old Testament we may as well at once direct our attention to a text, where literary criticism really has triumphed for generations, and has convinced many of the justification as well as the necessity of distinguishing between sources.

To be sure, it is neither impossible nor unreasonable to

[1] See the summary in Hylmö, *op. cit.*, pp. 103-126

suppose that in such an immense compilation as the Tetrateuch there should be certain parallel traditions, side by side or interwoven, each with its individual characteristics. In the telling, elements of parallel traditions may have been interwoven to form one narrative, and this may furthermore by its juxtaposition with other narratives have been furnished with certain genealogical and chronological data, connecting it with legends with which it may perhaps not always have been related. Parallel traditions may have been retained by the narrator with all their variations, for repetition, especially slightly varied repetition, is a popular stylistic trait, and repetition lays greater emphasis on that which is repeated. The narrator as well as the alert listener enjoys the minute variations that make reiteration more than a mere mechanical repetition. And if this is true of a dream or a scene or an episode, it is also true to a certain degree of an individual narrative where some feature is emphasized as important by such a repetition. It must be admitted that Genesis and Exodus-Numbers contain texts that are parallel and that have fallen into the hands of the editors of the Tetrateuch through individual paths of transmission. And it is just as indisputable that this same Tetrateuch contains texts where an older basis is sometimes apparent behind the present form. The merit of having established this belongs to literary criticism, but it is no more than one might expect at the outset of such a work as the Tetrateuch, that at one and the same time is a compilation and a revision of entirely different traditions. So far then it is possible to follow literary criticism: the material in the first four books of the Bible is heterogeneous, and the work as a whole presupposes a revision of the material in accordance with certain points of view.

On the other hand one can and must doubt whether the method by which literary criticism *finds* difficulties in the text and afterwards *solves* them is the right one. In other words one may doubt the correctness of the fundamental view and the methods of literary criticism.

(*a*) Its fundamental view. The narratives in the Hexateuch contain so many glaring inconsistencies, duplicate features, and contradictions, that one author, Moses or Ezra or whoever one chooses to name, cannot be responsible for it in its present form. Three or four or still more written sources must have been combined by various editors who have attempted the impossible and have sought by means of a mechanical fusion to create as well as they could one continuous account of time from its beginning until the constitution of the Israelite community. Even warm adherents of this fundamental view have recognized the improbability of this mode of procedure ascribed to the creators of our Pentateuch. However, if one does have misgivings of a fundamental nature, one will have to let oneself 'eines Besseren belehren', among other things by Tatian's harmony of the Gospels.[1]

(*b*) Its methods. The use of different names for God and the difference in style betrays the different written sources. Parallel accounts are distributed among the sources in accordance with criteria of style and contents; accounts with inconsistencies are analysed and decomposed, the different elements are distributed between the different sources, editorial connecting links are pointed out where their presence is considered possible or necessary, and after a thorough analysis the related sections are joined together and are then reconstructed to such an extent as the gentle treatment accorded them by the editors makes possible. Finally, a special character is ascribed to them as, for instance, naïve, popular, having anthropomorphic expressions about God, or marked by supernaturalistic theology, sober erudition, interest in chronology, or by reflective theology, cultural superiority, prophetic influence.

The literary critical work on Gen. 6-9 will be so familiar to readers of this chapter that there is no need for a detailed discussion of it. We will however quote a few things from Gunkel's commentary on Genesis.[2] From him we learn that a distinction of sources between J and P in these chapters is one of the masterpieces of modern criticism.[3] Indeed, the beginner can learn the method by which the distinction between sources must (!) be carried out by studying this pericope. First one

---

[1] Thus expressed by Beer in his commentary on Exodus, 1939, p. 5, *Vorwort*
[2] References to 5th ed., 1922   [3] *Op. cit.*, p. 137

should make use of the surest indication for the distinction of sources, the designations of the deity, and by this criterion a distinction can at once be successfully made between 6.5-7.5 and 8.15-9.17. In the central section where the name of the Deity does not appear in organic connections, it is necessary on the basis of the certain sections at the beginning and end of the pericope to establish a distinction and at the same time make use of other criteria. If one compares all the J passages it will be evident that the redactor has not included the whole J account (for instance we lack a J section relating the building of the Ark), but what remains is enough to characterize J as 'old, popular, naïve legends'. Whereas P, which is preserved somewhat better by the Redactor, is characterized by the sober spirit of erudition, by classifications and chronology. His Noah is not a living person, but only the pale type of a pious man.[1] And then one is surprised—oddly enough—to note that it is the 'sober erudition' that sets the whole mythological apparatus in action when the outbreak of the waters of Chaos is to be described (7.11-P), whereas the popular naïve story-teller narrates much more 'simply' that forty days of heavy rain caused the catastrophe. And as to the representation of Noah, it is in fact so little different in the P sections and the J sections that Gunkel can characterize J's Noah as an 'ideal of a pious hero, here especially a hero of faith'. And further Gunkel admits that J's 'appearance of Yahweh' in 7.1 is quite unsubstantial (i.e. neither popular, naïve, nor anthropomorphic), and that J's description of the destruction of everything living is colourless, and that an *older* tradition had described the Deluge mythologically (7.11 P). However, J also has very ancient traits: 7.16*b*, 8.21 f, as well as the sending forth of the birds.[2]

If one admits that a written source, the literary age of which is three or four hundred years younger[3] than that of another, contains features that are considerably older than the recension of the oldest written source, then one presupposes—as Gunkel does, too—that these written sources are the reduction to writing of century-old traditions, where the time of the reduction to writing in reality says nothing as to the age of the

[1] *Op. cit.*, p. 138   [2] Ibid., p. 67   [3] Cf. Gunkel, *op. cit.*, pp. xci, xcviii

material, but at most something about its last revision. This is a very fruitful point of view, but at the same time it deprives literary criticism of one of its favourite criteria. For according to this view it is impossible as a matter of course to divide the *material* into three age groups and to distribute the three groups among J, E and P. For here indeed the youngest source has an element which is older than the present form of the oldest source. External criteria, such as the criterion of the name of the Deity and the stylistic criteria, remain, but in that case source criticism indisputably loses its charm, the charm which it possessed when literary critics were fully convinced that source distinction clarified the development of the Israelite religion in the times of the monarchy and the exile.

It has been customary to consider the analysis of sources in the account of the Deluge an object lesson[1] to show how easily and naturally the source hypothesis was able to solve the literary difficulties in a text from Genesis, so easily and naturally that it might seem the only expedient; and so one is again surprised to discover, (1) that the hypothesis is only tenable when it occasionally comes into conflict with its own presuppositions, and (2) that solutions arrived at in a different manner account for the composition of the pericope in at least as convincing a manner.[2]

As for (1), we say that the point of departure in Gunkel's expositions (as quoted above) was the change in the names of the Deity. This criterion contributed to the establishment of the distinction in the first and last sections of the pericope. In the central section the reasoning was based on the data obtained in this manner and use was also made of the criterion of contradiction and that of reduplication. But what then are we

---

[1] Cf. Gunkel, *op. cit.*, p. 137

[2] In what follows I partly follow a work which, in my opinion, has not yet been accorded that place in Old Testament studies that a sensible, serious, *scientific* contribution to this century-old discussion deserves, viz. U. Cassuto's *La Questione della Genesi*, 1934. In Scandinavia it has been noticed by Engnell in his *Gamla Testamentet*, 1945, pp.187 and 191 f and *passim*. The story of the Deluge is treated there in its entirety from an anti-source-critical standpoint in ch. V, § 3: 'Il diluvio', pp. 335-353, the criticism of the criterion of the name of the Deity for this text in ch. I, § 5, pp. 40-45, the criticism of other criteria is distributed through chapters II and III. He maintains that our present Genesis is the work of one man, p. 395.

to do with 7.9? This verse tells of the entrance of the animals into the ark as 'Elohim' had commanded Noah. Hence 7.9 must belong to P. But exactly the same thing is related in 7.15, in a passage that on account of criteria of style and content must be ascribed to . . . P. What then is the value of the criterion of reduplication? Gunkel has seen the difficulty and 'solves' it by having recourse to a Redactor (in 7.9). It is reassuring and sometimes necessary to have a Redactor up one's sleeve. When the criterion of reduplication fails it is also possible to have recourse to other *terms*. Thus it is related no less than four times (7.10, 12 J; 7.11 P; 7.6 P), that the Deluge came upon the earth. Nobody will accept four sources for the coming of this deluge, and hence the critics speak of 'resumption' instead.

The criterion of the name of the Deity likewise does not agree with the criteria of style and content. In 7.8 we read that both clean and unclean animals went into the Ark. This 'pre-Mosaic' distinction between clean and unclean is ascribed to J. Nonetheless the verse is organically connected with v. 9 which as mentioned before ends with the words 'as Elohim had commanded'. Solution: Redactor!

Furthermore, it is maintained that one of the sources, P, is distinguished by its interest in chronology, and a very precise chronology at that, while the chronological statements of the other source are only approximate numbers, and moreover much smaller than P's. However, it has been known for some time that P's chronology in precisely this story of the Deluge contains an inaccuracy. He has the Deluge begin on the seventeenth day of the second month in Noah's six hundredth year. And it is finally over on the twenty-seventh day of the second month in the six hundred and first year. This curious length of time, one year and ten days, may be explained, if one assumes that the dates are based on the lunar year, whereas the object of the chronology is to have the Deluge last a solar year, the latter being exactly ten days longer. The culmination of the Deluge is reached on the seventeenth day of the seventh month in the six hundredth year, but the interval between the seventeenth day of the second month and the seventeenth day of the seventh month is by the same source set down as 150 days (7.24 and 8.3), though if the reckoning were according to the lunar calendar it should only be one hundred and forty-seven days. In this way the one hundred and fifty days become 'a traditional, inexact figure for five months', as Gunkel says.[1]

As for (2), however, if one thinks of the present text as more than a mere mechanical joining together of two different sources, i.e., as an artistic whole where old and new materials have been interwoven to form an account of no mean stylistic value and have been bound together by chronology, then it will also be possible to prove that the so-called J chronology (with forty days and seven days a certain number of times) agrees with P's accurate indications of time.

To be sure, the objection may be raised that 7.24 ('the waters prevailed upon the earth a hundred and fifty days') cannot agree with 8.2*b* ('and the rain was restrained from heaven'), P and J respectively; as the rain is expressly stated to last forty days it cannot very well have stopped after one hundred and fifty days. Those who have some knowledge of the Semitic narrative style will not raise this objection. For 7.24 is the conclusion of a section telling of the destruction of the whole earth. This section is very naturally concluded by an anticipatory remark to the effect that the whole catastrophe lasted in all for one hundred and fifty days. That it really is anticipatory is shown by 8.3 ('And after the end of one hundred and fifty days the waters were abated'). According to my opinion we have a similar anticipatory remark in 8.14 ('And on the twenty-seventh day of the second month the earth was dry'). In 8.15 ff we hear of the exit from the Ark, and of Noah's sacrifice which is answered by God's promise. As we shall see later both sacrifice and promise agree excellently, not with the twenty-seventh day of the second month, but with the previously mentioned date in 8.13, New Year's Day. On that day the waters were dried up from the earth, and Noah removed the covering of the Ark.[2] But 8.14 stands as the conclusion of the passage about the Deluge. The flood

---

[1] *Op. cit.*, p. 147
[2] I have already pointed out an example of an introductory note of this kind in the Deuteronomic literature in Jer. 36.8; cf. above, p. 67 and p. 72

came to an end on the twenty-seventh day of the second month.

We will now consider a few examples of how J's and P's chronologies agree with one another. On the first day of the tenth month the tops of the mountains were seen (8.5 P). Forty days later Noah opens the window of the Ark (8.6 J). This would bring us to the tenth day of the eleventh month. He then sends forth three doves, still according to J, and between the sending forth of the first and the second dove, and between that of the second and third dove there is both times a space of seven days. Now we read about the sending forth of the second dove that Noah waited yet seven *other* days, which would seem to indicate that there *also* was a space of seven days between the sending forth of the first dove and that of the raven that Noah had sent forth first of all. In this way J's information gives us a space of twenty-one days from the tenth day of the eleventh month, which brings us to the first day of the twelfth. It is hardly accidental that we arrive at a date precisely two months after the reappearance of the mountain tops and exactly one month before New Year's Day when the waters were dried up from off the face of the earth. According to 7.11 (P) the waters of the Deluge began on the seventeenth of the second month. In the verse immediately preceding this, we read that the waters of the Flood came upon the earth 'after seven days', (7.10 J). By comparing these numerical indications we arrive at the result that Noah went into the Ark (7.6 ff) on the tenth day of the second month, i.e. forty days after New Year's Day, of Noah's six hundredth year. A most attractive supposition is the one advanced by Cassuto, that the Deluge pericope once contained a note stating that YHWH revealed himself to Noah on New Year's Day in the six hundredth year and commanded him to build the Ark, and that this work took Noah exactly forty days. In this way we should by a combination of the indications given in P and J arrive at a reasonable explanation of M.T.'s otherwise inexplicable date, the seventeenth day of the second month for the beginning of the Deluge.[1] J's statement that the catastrophe

---

[1] The LXX has two other systems, and the Book of *Jubilees* a third variant. Cf. Gunkel's commentary, p. 146.

was caused by the 'geshem', i.e. the heavy rains, the winter rains, is in all its simplicity and naturalness widely different from P's mythological conceptions; still this statement may very easily be combined with P's dates if only we assume that the dates in these old texts are taken from Israel's old calendar which was able to hold its own as the sacred calendar even after the introduction of the Assyrian calendar, where New Year was coincident with the spring equinox. Then J's rains would fall precisely in December-January, the culmination of Palestine's rainy season. It may be possible that the account of the Deluge once existed in a simpler form with only the 'inaccurate' figures, forty days and seven days. In its present version the account of the Deluge does at any rate fit these numbers *cleverly* into a calendar that not only takes the natural course of the year into consideration but also places New Year's Day in the focal point. Let us in this connection once more emphasize that YHWH's promise to Noah (8.22), could hardly find a more fitting 'Sitz im Leben' than the New Year Festival in the autumn before the beginning of the rains,[1] the New Year Festival whose purpose was to ensure the proper balance between the powers and the perpetuation of life by ensuring rain and guaranteeing safety from chaos. In confirmation of this I wish to cite some words of wisdom[2]: 'The myth of the deluge, ending with the promise of the regular alternation of the seasons (Gen. 8.22), would fit in well with the autumn festival, all the more so since Noah who is saved from the chaos, reintroduced then, is the first vinegrower (Gen. 9.20). According to Lukian, *De dea Syria* § 13, the cessation of the flood was celebrated in the temple of Hierapolis by libations of water. The libations which took place at the feast of Tabernacles in Israel may, while they sanctified the water of the new year, also have been meant to recall the mythical renewal of the law of water as described in the story of the flood. In a Ras Shamra text, III AB, there occurs a myth about Al'iyan Ba'l's battle with the sea and the flood, i.e., the waters of chaos,

---

[1] This fits in very well with Elohim's promise in Gen. 9.8 ff, esp. vv. 14 f, 'When I gather clouds over the earth and the bow appeareth in the cloud, then I will remember my covenant which is between me and thee . . .'

[2] Johs. Pedersen, *Israel: its Life and Culture*, III-IV, 1940, pp. 749 f

which shows that an old Canaanite cult underlies the legend of the flood.'[1]

We have now tried to analyse a complex of tradition from the Tetrateuch, in order to question the certainty and confidence with which literary critics often speak of their solution of the literary problems of the Flood narrative. Thereby we have seen that a *mechanical* division of the text into two independent sources does not do justice to the present text. Such a division disregards the fact that our present text is a work of art, composed of different traditions, it is true, but in such a way that a unified work has been the result. Our main purpose, however, was not the negative one, to express our doubt and distrust of the method of literary criticism, but a more positive one, viz., to advance an alternative solution. Thus the question now arises: What is the exact bearing of our 'results' on the commonly accepted theory of the compilation of Genesis from two (JE and P) or three (J, E, and P) strands of traditions (sources)?

Evidently our results offer too small a basis for a general answer. A general solution of any value must be built upon similar analyses of the whole Tetrateuch. From the present analysis, however, some things may be stated:

(1) The author who is responsible for the arrangement of the traditions contained in chs. 6-9 has tried to compose them into a definite chronological scheme.

(2) If the chronological system has to be connected with P (to use the terminology of literary critics), it is no longer possible to regard this P as an independent source beside the older traditions or strata.

---

[1] For an attempt to understand Gen. 6-9 in its present version we refer to Cassuto's work mentioned above, though it invites criticism on one point: his treatment of Gen. 7.16 is flagrantly opposed to the principles he applies to the account of the Deluge in general, esp. 6.9-12. He divides chs. 6-9 into twelve sections where each section has its name for the Deity, § 3 and § 9 thus have YHWH (7.1-5 and 8.20-22), because God here appears in a personal, moral aspect, in the other sections Elohim, because God is there characterized as the preserver and almighty sovereign of life. But 7.16*b* (where the name of YHWH is mentioned) is thus left in an isolated position, and Cassuto inclines to adopt a conjecture supposed to be found in 'molti commentatori moderni', viz., substituting Noah in 7.16*b* for YHWH (*op. cit.*, p. 40).

(3) Nor is he a redactor. A redactor is a man whose main interest is in harmonizing traditions which he has neither created nor supported.

(4) He must quite certainly have been a great artist.

And now it may be allowed to put two questions which demand an answer:

(1) Is it possible to go behind this work of art and disentangle one special strand of tradition and to reconstruct it as a *literary book*?

(2) Is it possible to localize with some exactness in time and place the author, or the authors, of our *present* literary text?

If we were able to answer the second question in a convincing manner, if we could gain a picture of the personality (or theology) of the author(s), then we should possibly be able to answer the first question. We think therefore, that the next urgent task is the attempt at determining the character of our author, and this should be done by studying the *chronological system*, not with regard to its reliability as a historical source of information, but with regard to its literary character and theological (or ideological) foundation. And all the chronological material from the Tetrateuch must be taken into consideration, and not only the data belonging to the accepted P-source. The clue of this system, we think, is the clue to the personality of the author(s). Certainly, this task is attended by some difficulties, the most important of which are the divergences between the Hebrew, the Greek, and the Samaritan versions. These divergences, discouraging as they might be, are evidence of the great importance which was attached to chronology among the groups of Israelite people in Jerusalem, Egypt and Samaria.

INDEXES

(a) NAMES

Aaron, 41
Abraham, 40
Achilles, 31
Adonis, 34n
Adoni-zedek, 48
Ahab, 50
Ahijah of Shiloh, 54
Al-Azhar, 21
Albright, W. F., 44n, 55
Al'iyan Ba'l, 101
Alt, A., 48
Amarna, 30
Amaziah, 54n
Amos, 14, 15, 51n, 52, 53, 54, 76, 80n
Andersen, Hans, 18
Ar, 51n
Arnon, 49, 50, 51
Ashurbanipal, 20, 26n
Astruc, J., 12n
'Ataröth, 51n

Babylon, 29, 43n, 79
Baruch, 65, 66, 67, 68, 70, 73, 75, 76
Beer, G., 95n
Bentzen, A., 35n, 76n, 78
Bergman, J., 21n
Bethel, 51n, 64
Beth-Ephratah, 87n
Bethlehem, 86, 87, 90
Birkeland, H., 13, 14, 16, 52, 53n, 76, 78
Budde, K., 12
Buhl, F., 43n, 47n, 49n, 88n
Byblos, 16

Carchemish, 64
Cassuto, U., 97n, 100, 102n
Causse, A., 37n

Chronicles, 79
Covenant (Book of), 41

Dalman, G., 21
David, 43, 44, 45, 48, 49, 50, 51, 54, 85, 89, 90, 91
Dead Sea, 38, 50n
Deborah, 44
Decalogue, 41, 57
Delaiah, 69
Deuteronomy, 41, 43, 47, 49, 54, 56, 57, 77, 79
Dibōn, 51n
Doré, G., 63
Dossin, G., 43n
Driver, G. R., 26n
Duhm, B., 69n, 72, 73
Dürr, L., 26n, 59n

Ea, 28, 62n
Ebeling, E., 19n, 20n
Ecclesiastes, 61
Eissfeldt, O., 42n, 50n, 72n, 78n
Elijah, 43, 54, 70, 77
Elisha, 43, 54, 77
Elishama, 66
Elnathan, 69
Engnell, I., 14, 15, 17, 33n, 52, 54, 66n, 75n, 79n, 97n
Erman, A., 25
Euphrates, 43n, 65
Ezekiel, 61, 62n, 81
Ezra, 95

Falkenstein, A., 27n
Fowler, H. N., 22n

Gandz, S., 14n
Gemariah, 69

Genesis, 11, 19, 35, 40, 64, 67, 93ff
Gesenius, W., 43n, 49n, 88n
Gressmann, H., 19
Gunkel, H., 11, 12, 15n, 95, 96, 97, 98, 99, 100n
Guttmann, M., 21n

Habakkuk, 15, 38
Ḥabiru, 44
Hamath, 50n
Hammershaimb, E., 50n, 87n
Hammurabi, 41n, 43n, 53, 58
Harald Haarderaade, 32
Heshbon, 51
Hexateuch, 94
Hezekiah, 29, 55
Hierapolis, 101
Hiram, 45
Hölscher, G., 42
Homer, 31, 32
Horeb, 58
Hosea, 14, 15, 43, 52, 53, 54, 76, 80n
Hylmö, G., 83, 87n, 89n, 90, 93n

Immanuel, 87
Irra, 19, 62n
Isaiah, 14, 15, 38, 53, 72, 80n, 87n, 93
Išum, 62n

Jacob, B., 40
Jahaz, 51
Jean, C.-F., 43n, 44n
Jehoiakim, 41, 42, 64, 68, 70, 71

(*b*) TEXTS

Indexes